Numerology:

Discover The Meaning Behind The Numbers in Your Life & Their Secrets to Success, Wealth, Fortune Telling & Happiness

Table of Contents

Introduction

Chapter 1: The History of Numerology

Chapter 2: Methods

Chapter 3: The Meaning of Numbers In Numerology and How Numbers Work

Chapter 4: Getting Started With Numerology / Discovering Your Personal Numerology Blueprint

Chapter 5: Your Birthday Number

Chapter 6: Reveal the Underlying Meaning Behind the Numbers in your Life

Chapter 7: Guidance Regarding Property

Chapter 8: Having a Perfect Relationship with the Knowledge of Numerology

Chapter 9: Establish Your Business Based On Your Lucky Number

Chapter 10: In popular Culture

Conclusion

References

A SPIRITUAL START!

© **Copyright 2019 - All rights reserved.**

The contents of this book may not be reproduced, duplicated or transmitted without direct written permission from the author

Under no circumstances will any legal responsibility or blame be held against the publisher for any reparation, damages, or monetary loss due to the information herein, either directly or indirectly.

Legal Notice:

You cannot amend, distribute, sell, use, quote or paraphrase any part or the content within this book without the consent of the author.

Disclaimer Notice:

Please note the information contained within this document is for educational and entertainment purposes only. No warranties of any kind are expressed or implied. Readers acknowledge that the author is not engaging in the rendering of legal, financial, medical or professional advice. Please consult a licensed professional before attempting any techniques outlined in this book.

By reading this document, the reader agrees that under no circumstances are is the author responsible for any losses, direct or indirect, which are incurred as a result of the use of information contained within this document, including, but not limited to, —errors, omissions, or inaccuracies.

Introduction

"Wow! Wow!! Wow!!!"

These were my words when I first began to have insight into the mystery behind the numbers in my life. I had always thought various events that had an uncanny connection to my Life Path Number were nothing but "coincidences." I used to dismiss numerology as a "pseudoscience" only meant for deluded people, but I know better now. It is interesting to note that as much as people feel the knowledge of numerology is elusive, it is actually all around us. If you had been paying more attention to details, you would have realized that these "secrets" have always been staring you in the face, but you never noticed.

In the Harry Potter story, the favorite subject of Hermione Granger is arithmancy. This subject involves the study of the magical attributes of numbers. Hermione used complex magical charts to predict future events with numbers in the story. Arithmancy is numerology in the real world. According to numerologists, numbers carry immense powers and can give you insight into your personality and capabilities. I say "Congratulations" to you if you are new to numerology because you have been able to come this far.

I am sure that you have chosen to read this book, not out of mere curiosity, but because you want to have a better understanding of yourself. I am convinced that it is your desire to understand your purpose and make the best out of the life that has brought you this far. I can assure you that you have made the right choice by picking up this book. Why? Because you are about to be introduced to quality information that will change your life forever!

So many people go through life disillusioned and confused. They cannot make any sense out of their lives because they seem so close but so far away from living a fulfilled and happy life. They have had moments when things seem to be going their way. They had moments here and there when they had the world at their feet and seemed to have arrived "there." They really wish such moments would continue forever, but it has never been like that.

They experience so many moments of disappointments and heartbreaks. They have invested in the wrong business, made wrong marital choices, and did the right things at the wrong times. The wrong choices ended up almost defining their lives. All the good times they have had have been totally consumed by the bad moments. If the story of your life so far has been like this, there is hope where you least expect. This book is definitely for you.

You are about to join the league of millions of people across the globe living a happy and fulfilled life because of their knowledge of numerology. Just imagine how your life will be if you had a good knowledge of what to do when to do it, and how to do it. You will definitely make fewer wrong choices in your career and relationships with others. You will know the kind of people you should be with that will help you and those who are not beneficial to you.

Once you make more right choices in your life, you will have more good times and less bad times. You will invest in the right deals and make more profit. You will be able to take advantage of relating with the right people and all the dividends that come with it. You will no longer go through life, confused. You will be more in charge of your life. You will no longer be a victim of circumstances. You will walk a clearly defined path in life that leads to a clearly specified destination. It will boost your confidence, and your self-esteem will skyrocket.

As the saying goes, "Luck only favors the brave." Hence, the knowledge you will gain from this book is not to make you lazy. Knowing your "lucky numbers" and other amazing things you will learn from this book is intended to help you "labor in the right direction." Life is beautiful and enjoyable when you have a fair idea of what works and does not work for you.

This book offers you the necessary insight you need as regards numerology as a beginner. The essence of writing this book is not to add to your knowledge about esoteric jargon, but to improve your experience as a person. Hence, if you have a reasonable level of education as regards the subject matter of numerology, you are also welcome. I guarantee that this book will also add value both to your knowledge and your life as a whole.

This book is a step-by-step guide to numerology. Hence, no stone will be left unturned to ensure that you have complete satisfaction by the time you have finished reading the book. The information in this book is presented in a simple manner to aid your understanding. For beginners, it is important to note that numerology is not the same as number theory, which is a branch of pure mathematics. Hence, I don't want you to have the notion that this book is an "advanced study of mathematics." As much as there is a strong link between numerology and mathematics, numerology is not a branch of mathematics.

As earlier stated, this book is written to add value to your life. Hence, I urge you to treat this book as a sort of "gold mine," where you will dig out "treasures." These treasures are very vital information that will improve your life. Therefore, you should never treat this book as one of those books you read to while away time. You should not read this book just because you can't find any other meaningful thing to do with your life. You should read this book with the intention of getting the knowledge that will radically change your life positively. The study of this book is a journey that will initiate a new cycle of stupendous positive moments in your life. You will not only begin to have palatable experiences, but you will have them consistently. I am excited to have the privilege to be your guide on this great journey into the world of the mystery of numbers. The best part of your life is about to begin.

Are you ready?!

Chapter 1: The History of Numerology

The study of numbers and how they affect one's life has a long history. However, it was not until 1907 before there was a mention of the word "numerology" in any English dictionary. The usage of numbers to obtain critical answers regarding the purpose of a person in various cultures fascinated mathematicians. Hence, they began to investigate the veracity of these claims of finding solutions to human problems with names and numbers.

The Early Days

Pythagoras is often seen as the "father" of numerology because of his huge contributions to numerology. He was born in Greece around 596 B.C. There are few historical records about him because most people that wrote about him did so years after his death. However, few of his works survived, and his contribution to numerology is one of such outstanding works.

Between (A.D. 354-430), Pythagoras, as well as some scientists of his time, were of the opinion that mathematical concepts have greater practicability. One such philosopher was Saint Augustine of Hippo. According to him, the Universal language with which the deity confirms the truth for humans is numbers.

Just like Pythagoras, he believed that every event in life has deep numerical connections. Hence, the human mind has the task of understanding the mystery of these connections. Otherwise, the source of this understanding will come by divine revelation. The mystical connections between numbers and the events in the life of people made numerology gain wide acceptance across the globe.

Persecution by the State Church

However, the practice of numerology took a hit when the state church via the influence of the Roman Emperor, Constantine, banned the practice. After the First Council of Nicaea in 325 AD, belief in astrology became classified in the same category as magic and astrology. Hence, it became an offense to believe in numerology.

However, this threat from the church was not strong enough to wipe off the belief. Numerology still held sway as Dorotheus of Gaza did an in-depth analysis of "Jesus number." Jesus' number is 888, which is the natural number preceding 889 and after 887. Strong arguments have been made as regards what has a semblance of numerology in the bible. For instance, 7 and 3 are believed to have strong spiritual significance. The length of famine in the bible is often 7 years, and it took God 7 days to create the world. Jesus was crucified by 3 pm, and he inquired of God to avoid being crucified three times. The number 8 is often connected to change after seven years of drought. Hence, in spite of the ban imposed on numerology by the state church, it was impossible to make people stop believing in the supernatural significance of numbers.

Besides the Bible, there are also theories of alchemy that have their roots in numerology. An example of this is how that Jabir Ibn Hayyan, a Persian-Arab alchemist, conducted various researches based on numerology ideologies in Arabic Language using the names of substances. In 1658, numerology was prominent in the "The Garden of Cyrus," a literary discourse by Sir Thomas Browne. The author of the book was bent on showing that the number 5 and the quincunx pattern is present in the design, arts, and in botany in particular.

Other Contributions

Various people contributed immensely to give numerology the modern outlook it has today. In "Numerology, the Power in Numbers," the author, Ruth A. Drayer, says that Mrs. L. Balliett combined Biblical references with the work of Pythagoras. Other valuable contributions came from Juno Jordan, a student of Balliett, who gave numerology the Pythagorean system. This system was not developed by Pythagoras but by Juno Jordan in 1965 via the publication of "Romance in Your Name."

The book contained the modern system of identifying the vital influence of numerology in birth dates and names. Other numerologists such as Kathleen Roquemore, Dusty Bunker, Faith Javane, Mark Gruner, Lynn Buess, and Florence Campbell have all done their part to make the evaluation of events and personality with numerology possible.

The Various Forms of Numerology

Various forms of numerology have been studied and practiced over the years. Different cultures and dispensations have had their own form of numerology, which was prevalent during that period and in that culture. The Babylonians, Chinese, Japanese, Indians, Egyptians, and the Jews all have a form of numerology they practice.

However, the three major forms of numerology are Kabbalic, Chaldean, and the Pythagorean. Each of these forms of numerology has its peculiarities. Each one has a unique way of number analysis and interpretations. However, the common feature of every system is to help people gain insight into their purpose in life and events around them.

The Kabbalic Form

The Kabbalic form is based on the Kabbalah, the Hebrew alphabets. Hence, this form of numerology is rooted in Jewish traditions. "Kabbalah" literarily means "internal and spiritual knowledge." This implies that the knowledge is not derived from the senses but from your soul. In this system, every alphabet and number are believed to have a secret meaning that has practical application. The Kabbalic system deals with the birth name of a person in which 400 numbers and 22 alphabets are analyzed.

These numbers and alphabets are used to interpret the significance of that name and date of birth to the events that take place in that person's life. Each letter has a value that has a peculiar characteristic that explains certain aspects of a person's life. The Kabbalah form of numerology is the most difficult to interpret, but it offers great insight into the life of the person in question.

The end product of the Kabbalah system is to help you understand the talents you have. Hence, you will be able to put them to use and live a happy and fulfilled life. This form of numerology helps you understand your luck, makeup, and affection. Therefore, you will be able to identify areas of your life where you need to improve and be that man or woman you desire.

The Chaldean Form

The Chaldean form of numerology has its roots in ancient Babylon. It is the oldest of the three forms of numerology. The Chaldean system is often referred to as "mystical numerology." This form of numerology is named after those who initiated its practice. Just around the 10th century BC, the Chaldean tribe inhabited ancient Babylon. This form of numerology is often considered as the most difficult to learn of all the forms of numerology.

The Chaldeans are famous for their mythologies and prophetic capabilities. The reason it is considered tough to master is that its investigation is in-depth as it begins from a person's date of birth. This form of numerology is the favorite of people who are in love with ancient knowledge. The Chaldean system, unlike the Kabbalah makes use of 8 numbers – 1-8. Besides, it only deals with the name the person is commonly called rather than the birth name.

This form of numerology is not common, but it is known for its predictive accuracy and precision. It is based on the vibrations produced by specific numbers with their peculiar features. The outer influences in the life of a person are depicted by the single digits, while the inner influences are depicted by the inner digits. The Chaldean system tells you about your personality and your ideal profession due to your capabilities and personality.

The Pythagorean Form

The Pythagorean system was developed by Pythagoras, a Greek mathematician, and philosopher. It is the most common of all forms of numerology. It is also known as "Western Numerology." Unlike the Kabbalic and Chaldean system, the Pythagorean system is easier to master, which explains why it is the most popular of the three. The reason the Pythagorean system is easy to master is that it employs the system of the Western alphabets and numbers. Pythagoras believed that these numbers carry sacred energies that are incredibly powerful.

Concepts such as the Life Path Number, Destiny Number, and Soul Urge Number are predominant in this form of numerology. These numbers are used to make predictions about events that will occur in the life of a person. The formulas are quite easy to recall as they go with the numbers 1-9. The Pythagorean system uses a person's full name such that the alphabets of the name are converted to numbers. The numbers obtained from this conversion are used to get a destiny number, which is used to interpret the purpose of the person's life.

The Criticisms of Numerology

Those who are not convinced about the acclaimed power of numbers to provide answers to human problems have various sticks they try to use to beat numerology. Some argue that there is nothing spiritual about numbers; therefore, they have no ability to influence the incidents in a person's life. As long as such people are concerned, numerology is a mere superstition for people who are not ready to embrace scientific methods.

Those with the pseudoscience criticism will point to studies such as the ones that were carried out in Israel in 2012 and the United Kingdom in 1993. In the experiment that was carried out in the United Kingdom, 96 participants were involved. The aim of the experiment was to find out if there is a relationship between self-reported psychic ability and the number 7. At the end of the experiment, the researcher discovered that such a connection was false.

In the research that was carried out in Israel, 200 participants participated in the experiment. The objective of the experiment was to investigate the numerological accuracy of the diagnosis of learning disorders such as autism, ADHD, and dyslexia. At the end of the experiment, the diagnosis was found to be inaccurate. The researcher repeated the experiment twice to prove a point, but it was still the same.

Hence, skeptics will readily point out to such experiments to prove that numerology is nothing but a farce. However, as much as science has made life better by providing answers to numerous human problems, it is evident that science cannot explain everything. Science understands human physiology to a great deal, but science cannot provide sufficient explanation for death. Science has no explanation for emotions apart from pointing out the activities of hormones.

Hence, numbers and their significance is one of such things that science currently cannot explain. Numerology has played significant roles in history though critics would dismiss it as pseudoscience. Some scientists use "numerology" as a derogatory term for science they believe does not follow due to scientific procedure. For example, the coincidental similitude of some large numbers, which fascinated great scientists like Arthur Stanley Eddington, Herman Weyl, and Paul Dirac, was termed "numerology."

Such coincidences include the ratio of the age of the universe to the atomic unit of time, the difference between the strengths of gravity and the electric force of proton and electron, and the number of electrons in the universe. Funny enough, what became the popular periodic table today was as a result of what such scientists refer to as "numerology." The periodic table was formed through the categorization of elements by their physical properties after the discovery of the atomic triads.

In spite of the pessimism of some people, the veracity of numerology cannot be swept aside. I mean, you know that some certain numbers keep popping up in your life and they are affecting the outcome of situations in your life. A skeptic will dismiss it as mere coincidence. However, you know deep down in your heart that there is more to these numbers than they appear. I am sure that was what piqued your interest in reading this book in the first place. In the next chapter, we will extensively discuss the various methods of practicing numerology. The history class is over; let's proceed.

Chapter 2: Methods

In the previous chapter on the history of numerology, I touched the three major forms of numerology. However, just like I mentioned earlier, there are multiple methods of practicing numerology, with each method having its own peculiarities. In this chapter, I will intimate you on the Alphabetic systems, Pythagorean, Chaldean, Abjad, and mahadasha systems of numerology. I will conclude the chapter by comparing Chinese and Western numerology, and the connection numerology has to Astrology and Tarot.

Skeptics may say that the fact that there are different methods of practicing numerology shows that it is a false practice. However, researchers have various methods of investigating different research topics too. The experimental and correlation methods of research are used by scientists depending on the sensitivity and peculiarity of the research topic. Self-report methods and observational methods are also used to investigate various research topics.

Does the fact that scientists investigate various research topics with different methodologies make scientific claims invalid? The answer is obvious. Hence, the various methods of practicing numerology have their own peculiarities and practicability. However, every method is to the end that you will be able to gain further insight into your personality and talents. Numerology, in spite of its varying methodologies, has the unified aim of making your life more worthwhile.

Alphabetic Systems

The alphabetic system of practicing numerology exists in different cultures. The Arabs have the Abjad numerals; the

Hebrews, Armenians, and Greeks all have their own alphabetic system too. Before the adoption of the popular Latin Alphabets, the German Runes were also popular. The main theme of every alphabetic system is that a numerical value is attached to an alphabet. Most times, this system only requires the birth name and birth date of the person.

From the birth name and date, 3 to 10 numbers will be extracted. The numerologist will examine the birth name and the likely present negative influences of that name on the life of the person. In case the numerologist discovers negative influences in your life as a result of your birth name, he or she will suggest how you can minimize or eradicate these influences.

For example, you may be told to tweak your name cards or your email signatures. If changing your name legally will not be a problem, it can be suggested to you to change the name so as to improve your experiences in life. The numbers extracted from your birth name and date can also be used to discover your personality traits and talents. Both your overt and covert traits can be unveiled by the numbers extracted from your birth date and name.

The essence of these discoveries is to help you channel your personality traits to the career path that will guarantee your success. Your desires and passion will be unveiled, and you will be able to know your purpose in life. It is also fascinating to know that these numbers can also be used to predict what lies in store for you in the future. The opportunities and potential pitfalls will be highlighted for you so that you can have a fair knowledge of your options and the best decisions for you.

A typical alphabetic system numerologist will give you an opportunity to make further inquiries at the end of the session.

This will aid the numerologist to help you resolve any challenge you have as regards the assessment or other aspects of your life.

Abjad System

The Abjad system is the Arabic system of numerology. It is based on Abjad numerals or Abjad notations. In this system, each Arabic letter has a numerical value attached to it. This system is the foundation upon which "ilm-ul-huroof," the Science of Alphabet, and "ilm-ul-cipher," the Science of Cipher are built. The Abjad system has a numerical attachment to the alphabets as follows:

1=أ 2=ب 3=ج 4=د 5=ه 6=و 7=ز 8=ح 9=ط

10=ي 20=ك 30=ل 40=م 50=ن 60=س 70=ع 80=ف 90=ص

900=ظ 800=ض 700=ذ 600=خ 500=ث 400=ت 300=ش 200=ر ق=100

1000=غ

If you observe carefully, the alphabets are 28 in all. Each of these alphabets has a numerical value attached to it. This system of numerology has been in existence before the eight century. Abjad was actually derived from the first four letters of the Semitic Alphabet (A, B, J, D). These letters are also the first four in the Hebrew, Aramaic, and Phoenician alphabets.

The Abjad system is an alphabetic system. Hence, the essence of the numbers attached to the alphabets is to have a deeper understanding of an individual. The value of the numbers attached to your name has significance in this system. These numbers reveal your behavioral inclinations. They reveal your innermost desire and what your "calling" is in life.

From the assessment of the Abjad numerologists, you will be able to know more about yourself and the best professional path that suits you the most. You will be able to know the kind of business you can invest in and the kind of people that can complement you. You will have further insight as regards your strengths and your weaknesses. You will also be able to know what to expect in your life in the future. Hence, you will be able to prepare for any changes, whether positive or negative. You will have a clear direction in life.

Pythagorean System

The Pythagorean system of numerology is also called "Pythagorean numerology or Western numerology." This system of numerology was developed by Pythagoras, a Greek scientist. Pythagoras noticed that there is a connection between musical notes and numbers. He realized that the peculiar vibrations produced by stringed instruments have mathematical explanations.

The Pythagorean system of numerology depends on your birth name and birth date to reveal important information about you. This system attempts to explain your outer nature. Your outer nature is the personality traits everyone can see you exhibit. These personality traits are obtained from the numbers attached to your name.

This system of numerology works by first obtaining your name the exact way you have it on your birth certificate. Each letter of your birth name will have a number attached to it based on the ancient Pythagorean system from number one to nine. This system makes use of Latin alphabets such that the number 1 is attached to the letters a, j, and s. The number 2 is attached to the letters b, k, and t. Number 3 is assigned to the letters c, l, u;

number 4 to d, m, and v; number 5 to e, n, and w; 6 to f, o, and x; 7 to g, p, y; 8 to h, q, z; and number 9 to letter I and r.

The numbers that are attached to your full name as seen in your birth certificate will be added together systematically to obtain a name number. For example, if your name on your birth certificate is Anthony Martial Lionel, your name number will be obtained as follows:

Anthony = 1 + 5 + 2 + 8 + 6 + 5 + 7 = 34

Martial = 4 + 1 + 9 + 2 + 9 + 1 + 3 = 29

Lionel = 3 + 9 + 6 + 5 + 5 + 3 = 31

Anthony Martial Lionel = 34 + 29 + 31 = 94

Name number = 9 + 4 = 13 = 1 + 3 = 4

From the above calculations, the name number for an individual whose name is Anthony Martial Lionel is 5. If Anthony Martial Lionel decides to alter some part of his name, this will lead to a new number name. The initial number name is used to explain part of his life. Hence, an alteration will lead to alteration is some aspects of the individual's life.

In the Pythagorean system, your birth date is seen as an extension of your personality. Hence, it is also calculated to obtain a single digit. The number obtained from your birth date is used to unveil the talents or personality traits you wish you possess. This number shows the personality traits you possess but does not exhibit to the world.

It also reveals your purpose in life. It is important to note that in this system, there are numbers that are referred to as "master numbers." They are the numbers 11, 22, and 33. If, after calculating your birth number, it ended up being any of these three numbers, it will not be reduced to a single digit. The inferences about your life will be drawn from these numbers.

Chaldean System

The Chaldean system of numerology is also called the Babylonian numerology system. This is because it originated from the Chaldeans, who inhabited Babylonia from 625 to 539 BC. This system is used to identify the various changes in energy that takes place when you are speaking or when another person is talking. The frequency of the vibration that occurs when people speak around you varies and affects you and those close to you.

The Chaldeans use numbers 1 to 8. They don't use the number 9 because they believe that the number is connected to infinity. This system does not employ the use of birth name but the current name of the person. They do this because they believe that the vibrations that will be generated around the person are based on the current name of the person. Just like the Pythagorean system of numerology, the Chaldean system also attaches numbers to Latin alphabets.

However, because they only use the numbers 1-8, the numbers that are attached to the letters are not the same as that of the Pythagorean system. In the Chaldean system, the number 1 is assigned to the letters a, q, I, y, j. Number 2 is attached to the letters b, r, and k; 3 is attached to g, c, l, s; 4 is attached to d, m, t; 5 is assigned to e, h, n, x; 6 is attached to u, v, w; 7 is assigned to o and z; and 8 is attached to the letters f and p.

Hence, in the example of Anthony Martial Lionel, the name number that will be derived in the Chaldean system will be different from the one that will be derived from the Pythagorean system. However, this does not mean that the answer you will get from a Pythagorean numerologist will be significantly different from what is obtainable with a Chaldean numerologist.

Just like the Pythagorean system, the master numbers 11, 22, and 33 are also recognized and not altered. In other words, just like the Pythagorean system, if your birth name is 11, 22, or 33, it will not be reduced to a single digit. In this system, your first name shows the personality you present to the public. It also reveals your habits and personal interests.

Your Soul energy is revealed by the vowels in your name. This name is very vital because it reveals your innermost desires and talents. Your purpose in life is found here because the things your soul craves for is located here. The influence of your domestic family on your life is unveiled by your last name.

Mahadasha System

The Mahadasha system is a communication of numerology and astrology. "Dasha" refers to a state or planetary period. The Dasha pattern reflects the particular planets that will rule at specific periods based on the Jyotish. Jyotish is the Hindu system of astrology, which is also called Vedic astrology. Mahadasha is vital in the prediction of future events via the use of a natal chart in this type of astrology.

Mahadasha can create doshas or yogas that can change effects on transit planets. Anyone who wants to be wealthy, popular, or successful must have the support of mahadasha to make it possible. There are 9 types of mahadasha: Rahu Mahadasha, Chandra Mahadasha, Guru Mahadasha, Budha Mahadasha, Sani Mahadasha, Ketu Mahadasha, Sukra Mahadasha, Surya Mahadasha, and Kuja Mahadasha.

The grand total of all Mahadashas is 120 years life span. Mahadashas like Ketu, Sun, Moon, and Mars are less than ten years. However, Mahadashas, like Rahu, Saturn, Jupiter, Mercury, and Venus, are more than fifteen years. The effect each Mahadasha is determined by looking at the dasha lord, its Karaka, and its respective depositor as seen in the yoga-formation of the planet. The placement of Venus, for example, is important for the Venus Mahadasha.

A good or bad result is derived from the yoga formation during the mahadasha of the planets involved in the yoga-formation. The sign the Moon occupies is vital for the prediction of future events in this system. If the Moon is devoid of strength, every other planet is considered weak.

Chinese vs. Western Numerology

Chinese numerology is not based on just the numbers but rather the sounds they make when said out loud. Hence, if a number sounds like a word that is negative when said aloud, that number is seen as a sign of something negative. However, when the sound of the number has a semblance with a positive word when said aloud, it is associated with something positive. Therefore, luck is a key component of Chinese numerology.

The importance of luck is one of the major differences between Chinese and Western numerology. Western numerology is based on the Pythagorean system of numerology. In Western numerology, luck does not play a significant role. Each number has both positive and negative attributes in Western numerology. Therefore, in Western numerology is up to you to exhibit either the positive or negative attributes of the number associated with your name.

For example, in Chinese numerology, the number "1" has a semblance with the Chinese word for "honor." Hence, the number is associated with loneliness or independence. The number is associated with the water element; hence, it represents the ability to succeed in spite of the barriers in your way. In Western numerology, number 1 has a different meaning. The number represents creation or new beginning in Western numerology.

The positive attributes of number 1 in Western numerology include leadership, courage, and initiative. Meanwhile, negative attributes include impulsiveness and confrontational behavior. Therefore, while the Chinese numerology attributes the events in the life of a person to factors somewhat outside of the control of the person, Western numerology puts the individual in the driving seat of his or her life. Western numerology is very popular in the West, while Chinese numerology is popular in the east.

Numerology & Its Connection to Astrology & Tarot

Those learning Astrology & Tarot for the first time may find it daunting. However, it becomes easier when you understand the connection between numerology and the tarot. The deck of the tarot is divided into the minor and the major categories. Each of these categories is called "Arcana." The tarot deck consists of 78 cards. The understanding of the difference between each Arcana and their number will help you understand any card.

The minor Arcana deals with the physical realm, which divided into four suit cards, which contain the Wands, Cups, Pentacles, and Swords. The Wands represent will, the Cups represent emotion, the Pentacles represent material, and the Swords represent intellect. The minor Arcana has a semblance of the deck of regular playing cards but differs in that it has a Page, which is an additional court card. Every suit has a numbering of 1 to 10 and a corresponding element.

The Major Arcana are cards with large pictures, which represents vital moments in the life of a person. These cards are crucial and carry deep meanings when interpreted. There are 22 cards in the Major Arcana with the numbering of 0 to 21. The symbols on the cards of the Major Arcana represent the story of the transition from one phase of life to the other. It all begins at childhood and innocence and ends at maturation and enlightenment.

The numerological underpinning of the tarot lies in the numbering of the cards in the major and minor Arcana. The numbers on each of the cards of the minor and major Arcana have specific meanings, which is the core idea of numerology. There are five cards corresponding to the number 1: The Ace of Cups, Swords, Wands, Pentacles, and the Magician Card. The Magician cards are in the Major Arcana while the rest are in the minor Arcana.

The meaning of each of the four Aces is not the same, but they ultimately have the same message: new beginnings. Another approach to the interpretation of the tarot is to treat it as a cycle. The odd numbers generally represent instability and change, while the even numbers generally represent stability and endurance. The cyclical nature of the tarot is such that every ending depicts a new beginning.

Numerology in a Tarot Interpretation

In the tarot, the number 1 represents new beginnings as well as the first step on your journey. The minor Arcana Aces are the purest form of the element of every suit. They commonly appear when you are starting a relationship, a new job, or a desire to approach something with a new perspective. Generally, it is all about going in a direction that is not the same as the one you were going before.

The number 2 is the number of partnerships and the decisions you make on your path in life. It is during the process of consideration that number two shows up. This number demands the direction you want to take from you as well as the people joining your team. The number 3 is the number of growth. It can be the growth of a relationship, project, or idea. The number depicts natural progression and team building.

The number 4 represents foundations. This card depicts practicability and logical reasoning as a result of stability. The early burst of energy with which you started something important is now stable. This number shows up when you have achieved a level of success. The number 5 represents instability and change. This number depicts the struggles and conflicts that arise as a result of a clash of personality and perspective. It also shows up when an unforeseen challenge enters your path.

The number six is the number of relieve after a turbulent period. This card depicts that friends and family will come around to help out, and you will experience stability again. This card shows the importance of the support of the people around you to your success in life. Number 7 is the number of faith and patience. It signifies patience as you wait for your efforts to bring you the success you desire. It shows that patience and faith during the waiting phase are all part of creation.

The number 8 depicts progress and imminent success. The hard work you have put in during the previous phase of the previous numbers is about to pay off. There is excitement in this phase because you are close to completing the cycle you began from one. The number 9 is the number of completion. It shows that you have come to the end of a cycle. Your decisions and efforts will yield positive and negative results in this phase. The number 10 is the end of a cycle before a new one begins.

Chapter 3: The Meaning of Numbers In Numerology and How Numbers Work

Numbers are the "fuel" on which the numerology vehicle runs. Hence, it is impossible to understand numerology without a sound understanding of how numbers work in numerology. There is no number that is irrelevant in numerology. Although the meaning assigned to every number differs from one system of numerology to the other, ultimately, every number has its place and significance and has esoteric powers.

In this chapter, I will take you through an in-depth analysis of the workings of numbers in numerology. I will take you through concepts such as master numbers, double-digit numbers, and Karmic numbers. You will also learn about Palindromes and get explanations for why you keep seeing the same numbers.

General Guidelines

I will start with the single-digit numbers and their characteristics before I explain other combinations like thee double-digit numbers and master numbers. The foundation of numerology is built on single-digit numbers. The single-digit numbers begin at 1 and end in 9.

Generally, 1 is a leadership number. It is the number of creation from a spiritual perspective. It is focused on setting goals and not easily distracted. It has a knack for grinding out results. However, it is often unforgiving, impatient, demanding, and a jealous lover. 2 is the most cooperative of the 9 single-digit numbers. It is gentle, forgiving, and gentle. It is resilient and non-confrontational. However, it can be mean, jealous, and vengeful when others covet what belongs to it or mistreat it.

3 is creative and extraordinarily talented. A career in art is the best destination for such people. It has wit and excellent social skills. However, it is superficial and always wants to be the center of attraction. 4 is stable and strong. It is dependable, patient, and conventional. It finds satisfaction in personal progress rather than public recognition. They thrive in organized settings like the military but struggles in social settings.

5 is the most vibrant and freedom-loving of the single-digit numbers. It is always seeking change and relentless. It is daring and never submissive. It will never cheat on a partner like 2 and 6 no matter the temptation but can break a relationship easily because of the strong will. It felt free to date anyone when not in a relationship and annoyed if told to limit going out on a date.

6 is loving and caring, which is the reason it is called "the fatherhood/motherhood number." It is protective, sacrificial, and patient to teach. However, it is myopic and focuses on the smaller picture while ignoring the bigger picture. 7 is philosophical as it likes to seek and search the truth. It does not take anything at face value and places a premium on critical thinking. However, it is not honest and often opinionated.

8 puts emphasis on career, business, and power. It is a karmic equalizer that easily creates and destroys. It is generous and willing to take risks. However, it can be intolerant, aggressive, and greedy. 9 is special from a mathematical point of view. This is because if you multiply any number by nine, the addition of the result of the multiplication will give you 9.

For example, if you multiply 9 by 5, you will get 45. 4 plus five gives you nine. You can try it with other numbers. From a numerology point of view, 9 has global consciousness; it sees no difference between its neighbor and someone living in a different culture. It is the most tolerant and least judgmental of all the nine single-digits. However, 9 can be apathetic, arrogant, and cold. It can also be egoistic and immoral.

Double-Digit Numbers

Every single digit has its own peculiar characteristics and personality traits. However, sometimes, a single-digit number can be as a result of the combination of double-digit numbers. Such combinations often alter the personality traits of the single-digit number a little bit. For example, number 7 can be based on 70, 61, 52, 43, 34, 25, or 16.

However, their situations in which the change can be very dramatic in the case of a Master number or a Karmic debt number. It is always good to include a single-digit number that is based on a double-digit number in the numerology chart. For example, if a 7 is based on 52, it should be written as 52/7 and 43/7 if it is based on 43. The characteristics of a double-digit number are based on that of a single-digit number.

The double-digit number will retain some of the characteristics of the single-digit number and diminish some of its characteristics. However, it never totally eliminates the properties of the single-digit number. For instance, a 7 based on 34 is more creative than any other 7, while a 7 based on 16 is more withdrawn than a 7 based on 25. Numbers that can be divided by 10 without the remainder, such as 20 and 70, strengthen the characteristics. For example, a 50 is a high octave 5, and a 60 is a high octave 6.

Double-digit 10 is a high octave 1; it enhances the characteristics of number 1. This implies that the person will be a powerful leader with a sharp focus that inspires success. Such people can be ruthless in achieving their goals and have the tendency to become tyrants. Number 12 is highly creative, unconventional, and individualistic. They often have poor time management skills and poor team members.

People with a double-digit number 24 comfort and are adept in comforting and counseling others. They often like to play musical instruments with a particulate interest in percussion. They are often unstable in relationships and can be a bit gossipy. They will not be able to thrive in the absence of a solid, stable environment. Number 25 excels in spiritual leadership. It is the most cooperative of all the 7s but can be self-indulgent and too serious. They often find it difficult to share feelings and have a restless streak.

Double-digit 28 is a 10 but more tolerant and compassionate. It is a warrior number that is more determined and ambitious than the other 10s. 30 is a high octave 3 endowed with communication skills and creativity. It is a bit superficial but warm and possesses a good sense of humor. However, it can be easily distracted and lacks resilience and consistency.

31 is more fun-loving and extrovert than the other 4s. They are also more creative than other fours, but they often have issues in relationships. A key reason for their relationship issues is their lack of faithfulness. They cannot be trusted to stay committed to friends and partners in the long haul.

Master Numbers

All numbers carry significant meaning in numerology. However, experts in numerology believe that some numbers are more special than others. These numbers are referred to as **Master numbers.** In numerology, there are three master numbers – 11, 22, and 33. These numbers are not just powerful; they have added potential because they are combinations of two numbers.

People who have master numbers in their date of birth or name are gifted and possess special attributes that make them different from other people. Such people are unusually intelligent and possess heightened intuition. Each of the master numbers has its own significance and attributes accompanying it.

Master number 11 is the most intuitive among the master numbers. This number is often referred to as **The Old Soul** master number. People with this master number have an unusual connection with their subconscious and gut feeling. They possess rare insight and have the capacity to deal with sensitive situations with unusual calmness. They are usually relaxed in their approach to stressful situations, which makes others depend on them for inspiration.

People with this master number are prophets, clairvoyants, and psychics. Empathy and respect are strong attributes people with this master number possess in abundance. The negative attribute of this master number is that such people are in danger of experiencing fear and anxiety if they are not able to concentrate their efforts on a particular task. Popular people with this master number include Michael Jordan, Chetan Kumar, Edgar Allan Poe, Madonna, Orlando Boom, and Gwen Stefani.

Master number 22 is also called **The Master Builder**. People who possess this master number have an unusual ability to achieve set goals. They possess the heightened intuition of people with master number 111, but they are more disciplined and practical. Such people often have big plans, huge potentials, and great ideas. They have high self-esteem and leadership skills, which are the requisite ingredients for success. This master number associated with great thinkers who were able to fulfill their potential.

Such people know how to go about making their dreams come to fruition. They are often early bloomers with outstanding results. The negative trait of people with this master number is that some of them lack the practical ability to fulfill their undoubtedly huge potential. Popular people with this master number include John Kerry, Hu Jintao, Leonardo Da Vinci, and Will Smith.

Master number 33 is also called "The Master Teacher." People with this number are rare, as the number is the most influential and powerful. The reason for the immense power and influence of this master number is that it also contains the master numbers 11 and 22. Hence, anyone who has the master number 33 is an upgrade on the two aforementioned master numbers.

People with master number 33 do not have any ambition of their own; their ambition is to cause a spiritual uplifting of all mankind. Such people display total devotion and unusual insight and understanding without communication. They are more concerned about humanitarian projects and will give themselves totally to it.

Such people are tremendously knowledgeable in a very unusual way. However, they can be very emotional and tends to have bursts of anger. Popular people who possess this master number include Thomas Edison, John Lennon, Albert Einstein, Robert De Niro, Francis Ford Coppola, Salma Hayek, and Stephen King.

Karmic Debt Numbers

In numerology, you are perceived as a spiritual being that incarnates on the earth for the purpose of moving toward a higher state of enlightenment and awareness. Your long evolutionary journey has afforded you loads of wisdom such that you have made many right choices that have future benefits. In the same vein, you have also made wrong choices such that you will have to take on an additional burden to make up for the lessons you did not learn in your previous lives. This burden is what is known as a **Karmic Debt** in numerology.

The numbers that show you have a Karmic Debt include 13, 14, 16, and 19. The importance of these double-digit numbers when finding in your Life Path, Personality, or birthday is massive. Each of these Karmic Debt numbers has its own peculiar challenges and characteristics. For example, those with Karmic Debt number 13 will strive hard to accomplish any task. They usually have obstacles that stand in their way, which they have to overcome repeatedly. Such a person will find frustration in a commonplace and will be tempted to give up due to the almost impossible nature of the task to be accomplished.

Such people are often found to be lazy and pessimistic about life, but success for them is not actually impossible. They just have to work hard and be focused on achieving success in the task that comes their way. The reason some people with the Karmic Debt number 13 fail in life is that they are not able to focus on a specific goal. They focus their energy and resources on various projects such that they end up not succeeding in any. Such people will be tempted to take shortcuts, but they often have their fingers burned and can resort to self-pity.

Karmic Debt number 14 is a product of abuse of human freedom in previous lives. Hence, such people have no choice but to adapt to unstable circumstances and unforeseen events. They are in real danger of becoming drug addicts and the inability to control oneself when tempted with sex or food. People with this Karmic Debt number have to be courteous and modest to avoid going down the drain in life. Orderliness and emotional stability are also crucial to maintain focus during those periods of change for such people.

Karmic Debt number 16 points to the elimination of the old and the birth of the new. This Karmic Debt number is like a cleansing to remove every all that has been constructed to severe the person from the source of life. Such people have personal struggles with their ego and divine will. The grand plan of people with this Karmic Debt number crumbles such that they eventually learn to be humble to achieve true success in the long run. A spiritual rebirth takes place during this ruin, and the new person is born. Such people often look down on others because of their refined intellect, but that will lead to paying a high price to make them humble.

Karmic Debt number 19 points to the learning of proper use of power and independence. People with this Karmic Debt number will be forced to stand for what they believe alone. They will face difficulties but will overcome through grit and determination. Such people tend to reject the advances of others to help them because of their tendency to put themselves in a self-imposed prison. They find it difficult to come to terms with the need for mutual love and interdependence. They will end up learning the hard way that they can't succeed in life all alone.

Repeating Numbers

Repeating numbers like 111, 222, 333, 444, or 555 have interesting meanings in numerology. Each repeating number has its own particular characteristic and meaning. For example, 111 is a wakeup call from the universe. When you take note of this number, do a proper evaluation of your life and your approach to things. This number is positive because it shows that you are on the right path in life. It is a way of the universe, encouraging you to go on because success is within your reach. However, you need to be careful of overconfidence because being on the right path does not mean that you have reached your destination already.

111 also implies that you have the capacity to bring meaning and happiness to people around you. You have the gift of inspiring others and helping them achieve their dreams in life. Therefore, when you see this number appearing in your life, stay conversant with the way you are going about life and continue on that path. However, be also deliberate about helping others find the right path in life as you go on your journey.

2 is the number of relationships and partnerships. Hence, 222 is a clarion call to be observant about the kind of people you are allowing influencing you. It is a wakeup call from the universe telling you that your soul mate is nearby if you don't have one already. It means you should place a premium on valuing the people around you and reconnecting with your old friends. It can also mean you need to open up more to have new friends who will be beneficial to you. If you are in a relationship already when you start seeing this sequence of numbers, it means you have to be careful because the relationship is important, and you hold on to it.

333 is a trinity number that is pointing you to align your mind, body, and soul together. It is the universe telling you that an aspect of your life needs attention too, and fix. It may be that you have been too busy to pay attention to the needs of your loved ones lately. It may also mean that you are paying too much attention to a new relationship such that you are neglecting other important things in your life.

444 is a number meaning that you need to pay attention to people in your inner circle because "4" is the number of home and family. If you keep seeing this number, you need to consider spending quality time with your closest friends and family. It is a number also pointing you remember your roots. You may be missing out on some core lessons that made you who you are. It

may also mean you need to change the atmosphere of your home to make it more positive.

555 is the universe pointing your attention to the fact that you have enough momentum to move in a new direction. It shows you should be looking out for new opportunities, and you should ensure you are well placed to capitalize on them. This number shows that you should not resist change because the right time to move in a new direction has come. In case you have been waiting to do something new, you are poised to do it when this number keeps popping up.

Palindromes

Palindromes are numbers, sentences, or words that read the same, whether forward or backward. They include numbers such as 11, 44, 77, 111, 131, 151, 161, 202 etc. You may find something like 6:26 26% on your computer screen or $47.74 as the price of a product you want to purchase. These numbers have psychic meanings. These numbers are angel numbers with which your angel uses to get your attention. If you are able to pay attention to these palindromes, the mission of the angel is accomplished. You should not treat these numbers lightly because they have significant spiritual meanings to your past, present, and future.

Your spirit guide, which is assigned to help you navigate life smoothly, uses palindromes to communicate to you. The answers you are seeking about the next direction in your life are often right around you. If only you pay more attention to details, you will live a more meaningful and fulfilled life. A palindrome like 777 is the universe telling you that you need to do more than reading books but practice what you have been learning. 999 indicates the completion of a particular cycle of events in your life.

I keep Seeing the Same Numbers - What Does it Mean?

The universe has an interesting way of communicating with us through numbers. You can find yourself seeing repeating numbers on pieces of paper, a billboard, or zip code. These repeating numbers are pointers that something divine is happening in your life. If you often find a sequence of repeating numbers in your life, you need to take note.

The number may be single-digits, double digits, or palindromes. Irrespective of the number or sequence, it is a sign of divine communication. Your spirit guide is trying to point your attention to something in your life. It may be a part of your life you are neglecting or a part of your life you are giving too much attention. Numerologists help interpret these numbers so that you can have a clear understanding of the message of the universe to you.

The earlier you pay attention to these numbers, the better for you. You will make fewer mistakes in your relationships, family, and career when you have a good grasp of the message of your spirit guide to you. The great things of life are in those simple numerical details and sequences. Fools dismiss these numbers as mere "coincidences," while wise people dig deeper to respond to the intense effort of the universe to reach out to them.

Interesting Numbers: 23, 44, 666

Numbers such as 23, 44, and 666 are interesting in numerology because of their peculiar significance. People who have 23 as their core number loves people and are committed to promoting a good cause. They often freedom fighters, and they are the most creative of the 5s. However, they have the tendency to be realistic and quit when the going gets tough.

44 is a power number. It is excellent for people who want to have a career in the military or own a business franchise. Such people are visionary and always see to it that they accomplish any goals they set for themselves. Such people see opportunities where others are struggling and have unusual resilience, especially when the going gets tough. They are not fazed by challenges and relish taking the risk. They can think quickly and have the foresight to build something that will last in the long run. They set realistic goals and are practical in their attempt to achieve those goals. They are not just dreamers; they are all out to achieve their dream.

In the Bible, 666 is the number of the Beast or the Devil. Hence, if you repeatedly see this number, you need to be wary because it means that something evil is around the corner. 666 is also the number of life and mankind. The basis of life is carbon, and it has 6 electrons, 6 protons, and 6 neutrons. Generally, 666 indicates that you should be careful about the moments presenting themselves to you around that time.

Chapter 4: Getting Started With Numerology / Discovering Your Personal Numerology Blueprint

The greatest thing that can happen to you in life is to discover yourself. A very vital way to discover yourself is to discover your personal numerology blueprint. The knowledge of the numbers in your life puts you in charge of your life. You will hardly be taken aback by events unfolding in your life. You will be able to envisage events and prepare for them adequately. In this chapter, I will be taking you through the properties of numbers. I will also help you through how you can create your numerology profile and destiny map reading.

The Properties of Numbers

A major reason why the knowledge of the supernatural power of numbers seems elusive is that more people only have knowledge based on conjectures. Most of the things some people know about numerology are mere assertions based on mythology and not facts. For example, when it comes to the properties of numbers in numerology, some wrongly allude that there are "good" and "bad numbers in numerology.

In other words, such people believe that there are numbers whose properties are positive while there are numbers whose attributes are negative. Some allude that the number "13" is an unlucky number. As a result of this belief, some would not let their buildings have the 13th floor, while some are very pessimistic about the 13th of every month. They believe something evil will happen on that day to them or their loved ones.

In the popular scenario of the "Lord's Supper," some will point to the fact that there were 13 participants in the famous supper. One of the 13 participants, Judas, was the one who betrayed Jesus. Hence, some see this as further proof that 13 is an unlucky number, which signifies that even is lurking around the corner. Is this assertion really true? Is 13 an unlucky number? The answer lies in the true understanding of the properties of numbers in numerology.

In numerology, 13 is a "4" because the addition of 1 and 4 will add up to 4. Ultimately, 13 is one of the Karmic Debt numbers. Just like other Karmic Debt numbers, it is a number that indicates that the individual will strive hard to accomplish any task. It shows that the person will have obstacles and find frustration in a commonplace and will be tempted to give up. The reason for this is that it will be as though it is impossible to succeed in the task they have to achieve.

People who have 13 in their core numbers can be pessimistic and carefree about life. However, such people can be successful and achieve their dreams in life if they are determined and work hard. They will be able to succeed if they focus on specific tasks instead of jumping from one project to the other. Hence, 13 is not an unlucky number. It all depends on the individual who has the number as part of his or her core number to strive hard to achieve success in spite of difficulties. I guess you are relieved if you are one of such people.

Contrary to popular opinion, it is not true that some numbers only possess positive attributes, while some possess only negative attributes. In numerology, every number apart from zero has its positive and negative properties. Zero is a state of nothingness; hence, it does not possess positive or negative attributes all by itself in numerology.

Any number that appears in your core numbers, such as destiny number or life path number, possesses both positive and negative attributes. There is nothing set in stone in numerology. In other words, the positive or negative properties of any number or sequence of numbers that appear in your core number will not take place in your life automatically. In other words, you are the one who decides whether you will experience the positive attributes of your core numbers or the negative attributes.

Hence, numerology is not a magical practice that assigns an unchangeable future to you. In fact, you need to find out the meaning of your core numbers so that you can modify and change the events surrounding your life. Through the change of name, for example, you can alter the experiences of your life because your name contains the "code" that determines your talent and personality traits.

How to Create a Numerology Profile and Fulfill your Future Plans

Numerology is such that you can become an expert on your own. You can interpret the meaning of the numbers in your life and also that of others around you. You don't even need to be a mathematical guru or obtain a degree in mathematics to know the meaning of the numbers in your life. All you need is a desire to learn and explore. Once your heart is set to learn and make changes in your life and that of others, you are good to go.

The important numbers in your life include your Life Path number, Destiny number, and Lucky number. However, the most important number in your numerology reading is your Life Path number. Your Life Path is the road you are traveling in life. It is the "route" that explains the unique opportunities and challenges that will come your way in life. Your Life Path says a lot about your personality and the best career path for you.

You can derive your Life Path number through the simple addition of the day, month, and year of your birth. The day you were born was the day you stepped into consciousness. You began a new life, and all that you need to become all that you should become is already part of your DNA. Hence, every opportunity and challenge of your life are embedded in your birth date. If you are familiar with Astrology, a Life Path number is more like Zodiac signs you will find in Stars Signs Book.

If your birth date is July 7, 1995, for example, your Life Path number will be 2. How? The month of July is the 7th month of the year; hence, it will be represented by number 7. Every number of the birth year will be added together with the day and month to obtain your life path number. You will first obtain a double-digit number, which has to be further reduced to obtain a single-digit number. The calculation goes thus:

$7 + 7 + (1 + 9 + 9 + 5)$

$= 14 + 24$

$= 38$

38 has to be further reduced to obtain a single-digit number.

$3 + 8$

$= 11$

$= 1 + 1$

$= 2$

In a numerology chart, there are eleven numbers, which are 1, 2, 3, 4, 5, 6, 7, 8, 9, 11, and 22. Any number that is bigger than these numbers are added together and reduced to one of these numbers. When you live your life within the parameters of your Life Path number, you will feel energized and on track. However, when you are outside the parameters of your Life Path Number, you will be frustrated and unable to record any meaningful success.

Up next is your **expression Number.** This number is derived by the addition of the values assigned to your birth name. This number indicates your expressions in life and the best career path for you. Another number you need to pay attention to is your **motivation Number.** This number is also called your **soul urge number.** This number refers to the greatest desire of your soul. It points you in the direction of what you should become in life to attain fulfillment. Your soul urge number is derived by adding all the vowels in your full name together.

Your **Life Destiny number** refers to those things you need to accomplish to be fulfilled in life. It is derived from the addition of all the numbers in your full birth name. Your **Personal Lucky Number** refers to the number that will bring you luck in your entire life. This number is constant and does not change at any point in your life. You have to be careful because your personal lucky number does not indicate that something positive will happen whenever you see the number. It only implies that your chances of obtaining a positive result are high when you see this number. Your Personal Lucky Number is your Life Path Number.

Destiny Map Reading (More about You)

Every society has structures where they fit in every individual. These structures are meant to give both people who are present and those unborn an identity and a place in life. Unfortunately, many people are celebrated for their ability to fit into these structures perfectly. However, in fitting into these structures, many have lost their true identity. One of the worst things that can happen to a person is to do effectively well what he or she ought not to have done at all.

Many people achieve what many covet in life, but they feel so empty at the end of it all. They feel there is more they could have done and died in regret that they were never able to discover those things that were missing. The truth is that you don't have to wait until the end of your life before you discover your true identity. Thankfully, numerology offers you a "map" to your destiny. Numerology charts are the roadmaps where your uniqueness, identity, and weaknesses are unveiled.

Numerology charts offer you the tool to answer those difficult questions about your life. You have always known that there is more to your life than meets the eyes. You know that you are unique and have abilities waiting to be unlocked, but the knowledge seems elusive. An acquaintance with your core numbers brings an end to this almost endless search about who you are. Whatever seems hidden about your personality and the choices you need to make to turn your life around is closer than you imagine.

Numerology is all about knowing "you." You cannot claim to know you when you don't have a clue about the career path that is best for you or the kind of person that is best for you. Your knowledge of yourself is not complete when you don't know your strengths and weaknesses. Your numerology profile is complete when you know your Life Path Number, Soul Urge Number, and Expression number.

In other words, you have been empowered with all the weapons you need to go through life successfully. Checking through the numerology chart to understand the important numbers in your life is your ticket to your inner world. Once you know the path the universe has laid down for you to walk and your gifts, you are unstoppable. You will have clarity and know the exact direction you need to head in life.

Knowing the core numbers in your life may help you become a household name and reach unprecedented success. However, it is not always the case that you will attain fame and much wealth. However, one thing is certain; you will not end your life wishing you lived in different. The uncertainty and frustration that are commonplace in the life of many will be far from you. You will be convinced that you are living your life the way you are supposed to live it.

Fame and wealth are good, and we all desire to have them. However, happiness and fulfillment in life are more important than wealth and fame. What is the point of earning wealth and becoming famous, but you are not happy and fulfilled. There is no point living a life to make others happy and proud of you, but you feel empty. Hence, you should be happy with the fact that your knowledge of your destiny, strength, and weakness will give you an edge in life and live a happy and fulfilled life.

It is amazing to know that you don't have to pay a psychic or numerology expert to find out all you need to know about yourself. Numerology is such that any information you need is all around you as long as you search in the right direction.

Chapter 5: Your Birthday Number

One of the most important numbers in your life in numerology is your birthday number. Via your birthday number, so many important things in your life, such as your personality, career path, relationship choice, location, and business, can be revealed. Your birthday number is a code that says a lot about you. If you think the day you were born was a mere coincidence, you are wrong. People who were born with unfortunate events surrounding their birth often feel they are products of the mistakes of their parents.

However, every mistake is a blessing in disguise. You were not born mistakenly, even if it appears like that. The understanding of what our birthday number reveals about you will let you see how truly unique and special you are. Hence, in this chapter, I will help you to understand what your birthday number reveals about you and how that will help you appreciate your strengths and embrace your weaknesses.

Date of Birth Analysis

Your date of birth contains information about you that makes you different from other people. Your purpose in life is located right within the code of your date of birth. It is not out of place if you are one of those people in life seeking to understand the reason they are living. Life is all about expressing the reason for living. The intelligence for being is within that thing. All that a seed needs to grow into a mighty tree is within that seed. In the same way, all you need to become that woman or man you are meant to be is within you.

For everything in life, there is a purpose. Every change in season has its advantage and disadvantages. Many people don't like autumn because of the temperature, but that is the time for the harvest of many fruits and vegetables. The same way every inventor has something in mind for his or her invention; you are also on earth to fulfill a purpose. Thankfully, the universe has not hidden this crucial knowledge about our purpose in life from us.

What you need to change the direction of your life to live a happy and fulfilled life is located in understanding that you are. Your date of birth was the day you began to live as you took your first breath. Your date of birth carries the information about your purpose for life and the power in you. The purpose of your life is referred to as **the birth path** by Kabbalarians (people who practice the Kabbalic system of numerology).

The purpose revealed by your birth path contains the qualities embedded in you, which you have to develop through thinking. It also contains the success you are to achieve and the ideals you need to accomplish. Your personality trait, which is a combination of your strengths and limitations, is also revealed by your date of birth.

Your Birthdate Reveals Your Natural Talents

Generally, your date of birth is referred to as your Life **Path Number**. This number reveals your natural talents. There are abilities you get by learning, but there are some that are inherent. You may not discover these abilities until you are in a position to use them. Sometimes, you discover them when you are under pressure to perform.

However, you don't have to wait until you are under pressure to discover your natural talents. You can know your natural talents by knowing your Life Path Number. Every Life Path number has its own peculiarities. Once you know your Life Path Number and your natural talents, you will simply look for opportunities to show the world what you can do.

When you have a career that is in consonance with your natural talents, your job will become fun. You will not be under unnecessary duress to perform because you are only expressing yourself. Many people struggle to cope with work today because they are in a career that does not give them the ability to express their natural talents. Imagine Lionel Messi is a motivational speaker; he most likely will not be able to achieve the same fame he has by playing football. Hence, you need to know your natural abilities by knowing your Life Path Number.

Numerology Birthday Meaning Calculator

There are various sites that can help you to calculate your Life Path Number. However, you don't need to pay anyone on log on to any site before you can know your Life Path Number. You can calculate it by following a simple procedure. To calculate your Life Path Number, you will add the day of your birth to the month and then the year. For example, if you were born on November 5th, 1992, your Life Path Number will be calculated as follows:

$5 + 11 + (1 + 9 + 9 + 2)$

$= 16 + 21$

$= 37$

You will have to reduce the double-digit above to a single-digit number by adding the two numbers together. In other words, you will add the 3 and 7 together, which will give you 10. You will further add the 1 and 0 together, which will give you 1. Hence, the Life Path Number of someone born on November 5th, 1992, is 1. Simple, isn't it? You can try yours now!

What Does Your Birthday Reveal About You?

Now that you know how to calculate your Life Path Number, it is more important that you know the natural talents in store for you according to your Life Path Number. Below are the natural talents you possess as a result of your Life Path Number:

Life Path Number 1

You are result-oriented and a natural leader. You have a strong affinity for autonomy and independence. Your ambitious nature is supported by your discipline and determination to achieve your dream. You are never afraid of obstacles, and you "eat" risk for fun. Your courage and resilience will make others look up to you as a source of inspiration during tough times.

You are incredible, where there is a need to make tough decisions with calmness. You need to watch out for the tendency to always want to box others in and submit to your opinion. That tendency can make you a prima donna who will always struggle with group dynamics.

Life Path Number 2

You are naturally selfless and affectionate. You are tender and caring and always seek to maintain relationships. You are a natural diplomat and willing to make compromises to sustain the healthy atmosphere of any relationship. You need to be careful to avoid letting your emotions always get in the way of your decisions. You will also be an easy target for people who always want to have things go their way even when they are in the wrong. Hence, you need to add some "steal" to your tenderness.

Life Path Number 3

You are creative, optimistic, and love to have fun. Your ability to think out of the box and see what others are not seeing is impressive. Your relentless energy is remarkable and can dissolve negative energy with your burst of life. Your enthusiasm is contagious, and people will always look up to you to lighten up the mood during toxic situations. You need to watch out for being too "playful" when you need to be serious. All play, and no work is not beneficial, and you have to be careful not to get caught in that web.

Life Path Number 4

You find it easy to maintain personal discipline and adhere to a structure. Living healthy is easy for you because you find it easy to obey strict rules like a hygiene regiment. You want to live a simple life, and that can make you almost without any serious ambition. You don't like to take risks, and you need to bring a balance to this tendency. You need to push yourself to take calculated risks once in a while.

Life Path Number 5

You have an unquenchable thirst for freedom. You are adventurous and love to take the risk. You are always on the move, and that makes you struggle with structures. Your desire for new things is the basis for your unlimited creativity. However, you need to find a structure that works for you because you need a level of discipline to unlock your potentials.

Life Path Number 6

You are responsible and love to nurture and grow things or people. You are a natural teacher who is meticulous in getting your ideas across to people. You are a good link to connect people because of your mediation and reconciliation ability. You also need to pay attention to your own needs. It will be detrimental if you spend the whole of your time meeting the needs of others and totally ignoring yours.

Life Path Number 7

Your imaginative ability is superb, which makes you creative. You are introspective and reflective in your approach to life. You are intuitive and seem to be able to answer difficult questions. However, you need to be careful to be rational sometimes and not always move in the direction of your gut feeling.

Life Path Number 8

You have a strong affinity for power and wealth, and you will get them when you work hard for them. You have it within you to command great influence and affluence. However, you need to be careful not to be too materialistic. You need to avoid sacrificing your relationships for material rewards. You also need to be careful of being too desperate for power. It is not bad to allow someone you believe will do a better job taking the lead instead of you.

Life Path Number 9

You are naturally compassionate and tolerant. You are accommodative and accept people. People will always want to talk to you because you will listen to them and understand them. You have to ensure you are not too trusting and learn from every new experience.

Chapter 6: Reveal the Underlying Meaning Behind the Numbers in your Life

Meanings of Names

The numbers in your life are pointers to the message of the universe to you. Your unique characteristics and journey in life are hidden in there. In this chapter, I will take you through how you can translate your names to numbers. Why? The numbers in your names unveil your personality and capability. You will be able to know whether you are in the best profession for you when you know these numbers.

I will also help you know which lottery numbers you should pick, which increases your chances of success. I will also touch on your lucky phone number and 5 main numbers that can encourage lucky events to happen in your life.

Translating Names to Numbers

When the purpose of a thing is not known, abuse of that thing is only a matter of time. Your names are the "codes" with which the events that come your way in life are written. Your full name as it appears in your birth certificate is your **Expression number.** The vowels in your name reveal your **Soul Urge Number** while your family name reveals the kind of influence your family has on your life. Each of these numbers plays significant roles in your present and future.

Your Expression Number reveals your talent, abilities, weakness, and the likely hurdles you will have to jump in life. This number, as earlier said, is found in your full name as it is written in your birth certificate. How come? Your birth name reveals your personal history prior to the day you were born. Your birth name is not an accident because they are based on the intuition of your parents. This intuition is based on the vibrations created by your guardian angel around your parents.

Hence, when they finally settle on the names, though your parents may not even be aware, they will realize that they have been compelled by an unseen force to go for those names. Therefore, your birth names are the names your guardian angel wants you to have because of the impact of those names on the path you must follow in life to live a happy and fulfilled life.

Your Soul Urge Number reveals your greatest desire. It may sound bizarre because you may feel that you know what you desire the most. However, the shocking truth about life is that most times, you will never know what you desire the most until you find it. Some things you think are the most important to you right now will no longer matter when you find what truly matters the most to you. It is good to know that you don't have to wait until you find that thing before you know that is what you desire the most. So many people die without ever finding out what their soul desires the most.

Thankfully, the knowledge of numerology ensures that you don't have to wait before you know what matters to you the most. All you need to do is to find your Soul Urge number, and there you are! How? Just translate the vowels in your name to a single-digit number, and you will know your Soul Urge number. How can you do that? It is simple. The first thing you need to know is the value of each letter in your name. Below are the values of each alphabet in your name:

A, J, S = 1

B, K, T = 2

C, L, U = 3

D, M, V = 4

E, N, W = 5

F, O, X = 6

G, P, Y = 7

H, Q, Z = 8

I, R = 9

Therefore, if your full name as seen in your birth certificate is Abraham Quiroz Jorginho, your Expression Number will be calculated as follows:

Abraham = 1 + 2 + 9 + 1 + 8 + 1 + 4 = 26

Quiroz = 8 + 3 + 9 + 9 + 6 + 8 = 43

Jorginho = 1 + 6 + 9 + 7 + 9 + 5 + 8 + 6 = 51

After the initial addition of each name, you will then proceed by adding the three double-digit numbers you have obtained together as follows:

26 + 43 + 51 = 120

You will not stop until you obtain a single-digit number. Hence, you will reduce the number to a single-digit number as follows:

1 + 2 + 0 = 3

Hence, from the above calculations, Abraham Quiroz Jorginho's Expression Number is 3.

The Soul Urge Number of Abraham Quiroz Jorginho will be calculated as follows:

AAA + UIO + OIO (Vowels in the names) = (1 + 1 +1) + (3 + 9 +6) + (6 + 9 + 6)

= 3 + 18 + 21

= 42

To obtain the single-digit number, you will add the 4 and 2 together which will be equal to 6. Hence, Abraham Quiroz Jorginho's Soul Number is 6.

Discover If You Are In Your Best Profession Or Focus of Education

It is good to know your Expression Number as well as your Soul Urge Number. However, it is pointless to know how to calculate these numbers if you don't know how to interpret the meaning of the number. Hence, it is important that I help you with the interpretation of any Expression number you have. This understanding of the interpretation of your Expression Number will help you discover if you are in your Best profession or focus of an education.

Below are the interpretations of each Expression Number in Numerology:

Expression Number 1

This number is a leadership number. It shows that you have a natural flair for setting goals and maintaining the necessary discipline to achieve it. You are courageous and not afraid to take a calculated risk. You are ambitious and always see yourself at the very top of whatever you do. You are not cut out for being just a member of a team but as a protagonist. You are the poster boy of your organization and the energy that drives others to achieve the goals and objectives of the organization.

Your front-runner nature makes you an excellent entrepreneur. This number is also for religious leaders, elite politicians, activists, self-made millionaires, and inventors. However, you have to be careful of selfishness and pride. Your confidence in your ability is rooftop, and it may make you count the contribution of others as insignificant. You have the tendency to feel that you don't need anyone to succeed in your life. Hence, you are prone to dispensing people quickly and lacking the patience to help others grow at their own pace.

As a 1, you need to watch out for these weaknesses and maximize your strength. You must never forget that people are not the same. Help people around you grow, and they will never forget the positive impact you made in their lives. If you can successfully do that, you will definitely be at the forefront of great moves and business empires.

Expression Number 2

As a Number 2, you have the natural ability to make friends and connect with people. Most times, it is not because you are trying to be friends with people, but your likable and amiable qualities will draw many people to you. You have an open heart, and you are accommodative of people. You have empathy, and your compassion level is unusually high. You are quick to make compromises to "allow peace to reign." People with Expression Number 1, in particular, will like you to be their friends and partners because you are not confrontational.

Your diplomatic ability makes you more like "the power behind the throne" rather than "being the one on the throne."

Therefore, your ability is better suited for being a business partner rather than a business owner. You will be a valuable member of a board in an organization. You will be that link that connects everyone together and massage the ego of individualistic people to create a perfectly working group dynamic.

You will not thrive as much as you can if you are handed a leadership role. You will be diplomatic enough to carry anyone along, but you will not be able to make tough decisions without being too emotional. Hence, you have to learn to value yourself in your position as a supporting cast. No one can do what you do better than you. Hence, instead of envying leaders, rather appreciate your rare quality of being an awesome follower.

Expression Number 3

As a Number 3, you are outgoing, inspiring, creative, and positive. Your creativity makes you a perfect fit for a career in art. You are a social person who has so much positive energy around you. You can inspire people and make them go all out to turn their lives around without trying so hard. You have the natural ability to motivate people and turn toxic moments into positive ones with a snap of your finger. People will like to be around you, and you will have to learn to deal with this.

You will find it easy to attract the opposite sex, but you have to be careful to learn to define your relationships. Failure to handle the attraction of people to you will make you an unfaithful friend and partner because you will be trying to please every person that comes around you. Your natural ability to inspire people will be of good use as a motivational speaker. However, you may struggle to discipline yourself to concentrate on a particular objective for a long time. If you can cope with distraction and focus on your goals in life, you will definitely be a success.

Expression Number 4

Expression Number 4 is the number of discipline and structure. You are not flamboyant and thrive in obeying rules and regulations. You cannot cope when there is no particular instruction you have to follow to attain success. You don't want to be given the license to be "creative." You will be a successful accountant, government official, manager, or accountant. You will also be a good fit for a career in the military where obedience to instructions is the key to success.

You can still venture into a career in music and arts, but your touch of discipline and structure will still be evident. In your relationship with people, you have the tendency to be moralistic, which many will interpret as being a perfectionist. You may struggle to attract many people and will most likely have few friends. You will not be compatible with people who are outgoing. Only people who are disciplined or want to be disciplined will want to come around you.

You have to be careful because of your tendency to be a workaholic who will barely have any time for fun. Your serious approach to life will earn you many plaudits from your superiors, but you have to enjoy the reward of your hard labor too.

Expression Number 5

As a number 5, stability is not your strength. You are ad-free as a bird and love adventure, fun, and anything exciting. Revolting against structures is a norm for you. You will not only crave and fight for your own freedom all through your life but also that of others. You will be very vocal in your criticism of anyone or structure that restricts people from expressing themselves to the fullest. You will not be able to thrive in a setting where there are set rules to be followed, which inhibit creativity.

You need to be careful because your desire for freedom of expression can land you into trouble. You are prone to becoming a drug addict or any other unhealthy practices. Your ability to communicate will make you a good lawyer, politician, sales representative, or public relations officer. Your enthusiasm is infectious, and you will be able to convince people to buy into your idea easily. However, you need to watch out for yourself to maintain enough self-control in every sphere of your life.

Expression Number 6

Number 6 is the number of selflessness and genuine affection for others. If your Expression Number is 6, you are always more concerned about the need of others above yourself. You have a knack for developing a trustworthy relationship with others. Your friends can always count on you because of your honesty and faithfulness. You will easily stand out among other employees in your company as regards integrity. Justice matters to you, and you are never happy to see others suffering, especially for your actions.

You are very creative, but you may struggle to express your ability because you tend to have more time for others than for yourself. Hence, the time you have to develop your ability personally is limited. You are adept at reconciling people and psychological healing wounds. Hence, you will be at home if you have a career in psychology, counseling, and teaching. You will also do well as a farmer, florist, artist, designer, or gardener.

A career in business is not also out of place for you, especially in areas where human relations are very vital. You have to ensure you maintain a balance between the time you spend on helping others and cultivating your own abilities to thrive.

Expression Number 7

7 is the number of truth, knowledge, and analysis. If your Expression Number is 7, your desire for knowledge will be insatiable. Critical life issues that many consider as mysterious will be your focus. You will want to be the one people can look up to for answers to difficult questions. Your analytical skill is excellent, and your ability for logical reasoning is difficult to match. You have the tendency to keep your thoughts to yourself until you are convinced that the time is right for you to tell others.

A career in science or philosophy will be perfect for you. You will thrive as an analyst, researcher, inventor, lawyer, priest, or banker. Your love for mysticism and investigation will also come in handy as a detective. You have to watch out for too much of keeping your thoughts to yourself. You may find it difficult to connect with people because they will find you too mysterious and secretive. People will feel you are unpredictable, and it can affect your interpersonal relationship because you will be classified as an undependable person.

Your depth of knowledge will also paint you as someone who is too critical of others. Hence, learn to take out time to reflect on your actions. Dismiss falsehood but let it be clear to people that you are attacking their wrong assertions and not their personality.

Expression Number 8

People who have Expression number 8 are designed for the pinnacle of their career. They are fiercely competitive and have the discipline and focus on becoming the very best in whatever they do. Influence and affluence are within their domain. They are great achievers who can break and set records for fun. They will face great challenges, but they are equipped to surmount every challenge and come out tops. The challenges they face will only make them realize their immeasurable potential to succeed.

They are easy choices for leadership positions. A career as an entrepreneur is perfect for such people. They are business owners and have the ability to create a business dynasty that has global coverage. Their focus and discipline make them impossible to stop from attaining their goals. They set the standard for others to follow. However, they have to be careful not to be self-conceited and intolerant of others. Their ability to be focused and achieve their goals can make them treat others as irrelevant.

Expression Number 9

This is the number of humanitarian services, compassion, and idealism. If you have this number as your Expression Number, you have a global view of the world. You want everyone in the world to see themselves as the same and not see any race as inferior. You have the intention to change the world and make it a better place. You have your greatest moment of satisfaction whenever you do something that affects others. A career in law, politics, teaching, or medicine will be a perfect fit for you. Your desire to light up others and alleviate their pain will be needed there.

Prejudice does not have any place with you. You project a cool and loving image to people, and that will draw many people to you. However, you usually don't express what you feel. You believe strongly in the good of humanity, but you are poor in judging the character of people.

Know Your Lucky Mobile Number

On 31st of October 2016, a post on *Bangkok Post* was written on "Extremely Lucky phone numbers could fetch B100 million". According to this post, there were four companies that expressed an interest in bidding for these 16 lucky phone numbers. Why will companies be ready to path away with their hard-earned money for "fun"? Hence, it shows that some mobile numbers actually attract luck to the owners.

According to the post, the 16 phone numbers include 099- 999- 9999, 088- 888- 8888, 090- 000- 0000, 091- 111- 1111, 092- 222- 2222, 093- 333- 3333, 094- 444- 4444, 095- 555- 555, 096- 666- 6666, 097- 777- 7777, 098- 888- 8888, 061- 111- 1111, 062- 222- 2222, 063- 333- 3333, 064- 444- 4444, and 065- 555- 5555.

These companies want to purchase these numbers because they are both easy to remember and bring luck to the owners. The reason for the ability of these numbers to bring luck is primarily because these numbers have a semblance with Chinese names for prosperity and other good things of life. Besides, the sequence of these numbers shows a conglomeration of particular numbers. The positive energies of the conglomeration of a particular number will attract good tidings to the owners of these numbers.

Hence, when choosing a mobile number, consider a phone number that has a particular number being repeated. Such phone numbers will improve the rate at which you have lucky events come your way. When it comes to numerology, as much as nothing is set in stone, you also cannot afford to take anything for granted. A little tweak of numbers can change your experience in life. If things are not working and you are not ready to try something new, you are not doing yourself any good.

Hence, always look out for means of improving your general approach in life, but don't forget to look out for the numbers too. You may be doing exactly what you need to succeed but just have unlucky numbers in your life. It will now look as though you are not working hard enough like your peers; meanwhile, the issue is that you have not had favorable events come your way.

Five Main Numbers that can Encourage Lucky Events to Happen in your Life

Finding lucky numbers in your life is not just real; it is also fun. Every number in the numerological perspective has both positive and negative attributes. However, there are some particular numbers that can encourage lucky events to happen in your life. These numbers will help you with which lottery numbers you should choose.

The first number you should consider is your **Life Path Number**. I have discussed how to calculate it in the previous chapter. It is derived from your date of birth. This number resonates with you and will bring you luck. You can also go with a traditionally lucky number like 7, 3, or 4. Alex Bellos, a mathematician, ran a poll to discover the most popular lucky number in the world. The result of the poll showed that number 7 is the most popular lucky number in the world.

It is not too surprising because the number 7 is quite significant. There are 7 days of the week, 7 continents, 7 seas and other interesting, fun facts. Good things also come in threes and fours. However, you need to be careful about using traditional numbers because there will be many other people using them.

Hence, in case you win a jackpot, you are likely to split it. If you have kids, you can also consider the date of birth of your kids.

NB: Never forget that these numbers only gives you a higher chance of winning and not absolute. Any number can make you win a lottery. Hence, don't bet money you cannot afford to lose because you are placing money on a lucky number. That will not be too wise of you.

Chapter 7: Guidance Regarding Property

Every location on earth has peculiar characteristics that make people decide to live there. For some people, they prefer environments where there are a lot of people so that they can have more than enough social interactions daily. For others, they cannot afford to have "noisy neighbors." For such people, even if they don't have enough money to live in such residential areas, it is their dream to live there someday.

It is normal for you to consider various factors such as the safety of your life and properties, economic activities of the location, and proximity to your place of work. However, those factors are not enough bases for your choice of location. You can actually take advantage of your knowledge of numerology when choosing the location of your home or business. In this chapter, I will be taking you through how you can make your life better by choosing your address with numerology in mind.

When Choosing a New Home, should one use Numerology?

Yes. Why? In numerology, numbers are everything. Just like your birth date, your address has numbers associated with it. Never forget that every number in numerology has both positive and negative attributes. Hence, the address of your home or company has both positive and negative attributes that will affect your experiences. Therefore, you cannot afford to sideline numerology when making your choice as regards the address of your home or business.

If you have just moved to a new home, it is important you find out the Home Number of your new address. Knowing this number will help you know what to expect and prepare for future events. You will also be able to make quality decisions as regards staying in that address or leaving the place for somewhere better.

The first thing you need to do know the personality of your home is to know the Number of your home. When I say, "Number of your home," I am not talking about the address of your home but the numerological number of your home. This number reveals the peculiar character and energy of your home. It is not difficult to know this number. The only issue you may have is that there are particular cases in which the number you will focus on will be different. Once you can master the rule for each case, you are good to go.

You need to disassemble and add your address together to know this number. For instance, if your address is at "798 Main Street", you will take out the numbers and add them together as follows:

$7 + 9 + 8 = 24$

If you get a double-digit, you will have to reduce it to a single-digit further to unveil the unique character and energy of your home as follows:

$2 + 4 = 6$

From the above calculation, the numerological representation of your home is 6. Easy, isn't it? You can try yours right now. It is fun! However, you may seemingly encounter a challenge if the name of your street is number. I mean, if your address is something like "560 6th Avenue". You will be tempted to add the number 6 in the 6th to the 560, but that will not be correct. If your address is in this form, you will ignore the name of the street. I mean, you will only add the numbers together as follows:

5 + 6 + 0 = 11

Just like the last example, you will further reduce the double-digit to a single-digit number by adding the numbers together as follows:

1 + 1 = 2

That means your Home Number is 2 in such instance. If you live in an apartment, the method will be a little bit different again. The difference is that the focus is not the same. However, the technique of addition and reduction of double-digit to obtain a single-digit is still the same. You will have to use your unit number in case of an apartment. Your unit number is a unique number for your space.

In case your address is something like "1700 Harry Court, Apt 45", you will ignore the "1700" in front of the apartment address. You will only concentrate on the "45" at the end of the address because that is your unit number. The addition of the two numbers will be equal to 9. It is possible that your address is a little different from the three scenarios that have been addressed so far. It is possible that your apartment or street number contains a letter. I mean, if your street or apartment number is something like "876B,".

In such a situation where there is a letter attached to your street or apartment number, don't ignore the letter! Any Home Number you obtain through the elimination of the letter in such a situation is inaccurate. Before adding the numbers together, you will have to obtain the number equivalent of the letter in the Pythagorean System of Numerology. The number equivalent of letter B in this system is 2.

Note: The full representation of letters with their respective numbers can be found in chapter 6 of this book.

Therefore, if your address is 876B Willow Avenue, your Home Number will be calculated as follows:

8 + 7 + 6 + 2 = 23

Further reduction of the number will lead to the addition of 2 and 3, which will be equal to 5. Hence, your Home number, in that case, will be 5. As have seen, knowing your Home number is not difficult. The only reason why it may seem complicated in some instances is when you don't know the exact rule that applies to the addition of numbers.

How The Address of Your Home Affects You

Now that you know how to obtain your Home Number, it is important to know the implication of your own Home Number. As earlier said, every number has its own peculiar energy and characteristic. Below are the characteristics of each Home Number from 1 to 9.

Home Number 1

1 stand for strength, innovation, and independence. The number one Home Number is perfect for single people or entrepreneurs. This Home Number supports their need for independence, personal freedom, and autonomy. The energy this number oozes supports the desire to explore and break new grounds. If you are about to or just began a new business, you need to consider an address with this number.

1 feeds you with the energy for the requisite self-confidence to channel your resources in the right direction. Hence, if you desire a life partner anytime soon, you have to desist from living in an address whose Home Number is 1. The energy of this address is all about you and will even affect your chances of starting or maintaining a healthy relationship.

If you have a family already and you are living in this address, you need to consider relocation as fast as possible. The energy of this address does not support the soft and interdependence nature of a family. You don't have to cause trouble in your home by pushing so hard for relocation without carrying others along, especially your partner. Let him or she knows that the happiness of the family is the driving force behind your insistence on relocation.

Home Number 2

A family person leaving an address with Home Number 1 will find an address with Home Number two, a perfect place to grow and nurture a family. The energy of 2 supports building a home to give every member of the family a sense of belonging. If there is an address that is the complete opposite of 1, it is 2. The major difference between two and 1 is that 2 is meant for interpersonal relationships where group dynamics supersedes individualism.

The energy of 2 is perfect for loving relationships and harmonious living. Young families, romantic partners, and roommates who have cordial relationships will enjoy a Home Number 2 address. They will be comfortable there because the energy of the home supports sentiments and sensitivity, which are backbones of cordial relationships.

However, just like every number in numerology, 2 has its negative impacts too. The fact that the energy it oozes supports a family and group structure makes it detrimental to people who thrive on creativity and individual brilliance. If you want to focus on creating a business or single and not interested in building a family anytime soon, 3 is not a good address for you.

Home Number 3

3 is the hub of entertainment and creativity. If you are into a career where the premium is placed on creativity, this is the best home for you. The vibrations of this home provide the much-needed platform for expression and creation of new things. Hence, if you are an artist or involved in a career where expressing yourself in a new and dynamic way is paramount, the energy of 3 suits you perfectly.

3 is also cut out for social gatherings and squeezing as much fun as possible out of life. Hence, if you are the kind of person who likes having interesting people come around you regularly for parties and great times, 3 is your best bet. However, you need to be careful because this number can move you closer to bankruptcy. With much fun and entertainment comes the desire to spend lavishly on liabilities.

Hence, if you have a plan to live a serene life devoid of distraction and extravagance, 3 is not healthy for you. Hence, before you make the decision to live in a Home Number 3 address, you need to decide what matters to you between having maximum fun and living a shrewd, sober life.

Home Number 4

Home Number 4 is the center of discipline and responsibility. Just as 1 is the opposite of 2, 3 is the opposite of 4. The vibration of 4 supports living a discipline, grounded, and responsible life. It does not support fun and extravagance. 4 is perfect for people who want to raise responsible kids and steadily grow their business. The abundance of energy for structure and discipline makes this home a "taboo" for people who love to have a lot of friends come around them often for entertainment.

Therefore, you are adventurous and like to be a little "wild," you will be making a mistake by choosing to live in 5. The energy of 5 supports a stable structure, which is also beneficial if you want to have a home garden. For a low key life where growth and stability are at the top of your list, let an address whose Home Number is 4 be non-negotiable for you. You will struggle to find your feet, and your life will be like that of a fish on the dry ground if you live in 3.

Home Number 5

Just like 3, 5 is a vibrant house for social life. If you have a knack for inviting people to come to your house and have nice times, 5 is suitable for you. The energy of this number resonates with social activities and entertainment. Unlike 3, it does not ooze out the energy for creativity as such but for variety and change. However, the fact that this house promotes variety and instability can be a problem for you. You may find it difficult to live in that house for long.

When you live in this house, circumstances around you will make you want to leave the house and go elsewhere. Hence, if you are looking for a place you can stay for a long time in harmony with your family and proximity to your workplace, 5 is not an ideal home for you. Apart from the vibrant social life, 5 also has the added advantage of making you bold and fearless. The energy of this home gives you the confidence to handle tough situations and come out a winner.

Therefore, you can be sure that by the time you decide to leave the house, you would have learned a lot of lessons in life. 5 is a perfect house to train yourself to be strong and courageous in life to face difficult tasks. Hence, 5 is a perfect stopover for single people before they move on to stability with a family in a Home Number 2 house.

Home Number 6

Home number 6 is similar to Home Number 6 because they both support harmonious living for families. In numerology, 6 is the number that supports homeliness and family setting the most. The energy of 6 makes people feel welcome and at home. Not only you and your family will feel welcome in this home, your guests, too, will feel welcome here. In fact, your pets will enjoy the atmosphere of the home. It is just the perfect sanctuary for a settled, peaceful, and warm setting of love and harmony.

To appreciate the nature of the home, decorate it with nice pictures and comfortable furniture. Flowers and a home garden will also be perfect for this home. Of course, living in a home-like this is not good, for you want to embrace a single life for the time being. The energy will be detrimental to your desire to be independent and enjoy your freedom.

In this home, you will find yourself wanting, and circumstances around you will arrange themselves to get you engaged. You will have to keep running away from "settling down" if you live in a home-like this. Hence, if you are not ready for the responsibility that comes with the stability and interdependence of having a family, 6 is not a good home for you.

Home Number 7

7 is a sanctuary for a quiet, spiritual, and sober life. If you are the kind of person who wants your home to be a haven to stay away from the "noisy world," 7 is your perfect "hideout." The energy of this home inspires deep thought and reflection and can be somewhat secretive. If you are not the kind of person who thrives on simplicity in your approach to life, you will be living in the wrong home if you find yourself in this home.

You will have to simplify your goals and ambition in life, or else, the energy of this home will feel "choking" for you. You will have to remove any clutter from your thought and environment to be able to live in this home without any issue. You need to connect with the energy of this home to feel at home here. 7 is the perfect home for writers or scientists because of their need to have a clear mind for optimum performance.

The energy of this home ensures that you will be able to know yourself as you reflect on your past actions. It will help you make clear, concrete plans about the future and prepare to be a better person in the future. Meditation is a free flow because of the vibration of Home Number 7.

Home Number 8

8 is quite popular because of its energy for prosperity and abundance. The energy of this home supports growth and ambition, which is necessary for success in business. Hence, an entrepreneur or people who have the drive to reach the pinnacles of their career will find 8 a perfect home for them. Hence, if it is very crucial for you to increase your status in life and attain financial independence, this is your best bet.

8 supports growth, and even growth in family size comes with ease here. However, the energy of 8 for growth is not without its detriment. It does not support stability and relaxation; it is all about the increase and upward movement. Therefore, 8 is not a good choice for you if it is more important for you that you have a stable and relaxed atmosphere in your home. The upward movement of 8 brings with it a raucous atmosphere that is not healthy for a happy and harmonious home.

A simple rule of numerology is that you can't eat your cake and have it. You will have to choose the characteristics that are top of your list before you decide which home is best for you.

Home Number 9

The last but not the least is Home Number 9. This is the number of acceptance, compassion, and reality. The energy of this number attracts everyone in the world. In another world, this number does not permit discrimination among people of different races and languages. It is an accommodative number, also called the "International number." The vibe around this home promotes selflessness, forgiveness, spirituality, and creativity.

If you have a global view of making the world a better place through selfless sacrifices and humanitarian services, 9 is the best home for you. The energy this home ooze will help you learn a lot about yourself, and you are inspired to live a life that will leave an indelible mark on human history. If you live in this home, you have to be accommodative and tolerant of being in tandem with the vibration of this home.

Your heart should be opened to all, not for the fun of having people come around you but to make a meaningful impact in the lives of people. People will see you as a source of inspiration and a great example to humanity when you resonate with the energy of this home.

Chapter 8: Having a Perfect Relationship with the Knowledge of Numerology

As you would have noticed by now, the knowledge of numerology can help you in every aspect of your life. In this chapter, I will be narrowing down on the application of the knowledge of numerology to your marital relationship. Well, a perfect relationship is not a relationship where there are no issues. A perfect relationship is a relationship where the couples understand themselves and are willing to make compromises for the sake of the relationship. I don't want you to switch off or flip the pages over because you are already in a relationship. This is because this chapter is not only for people who are single but also for people who are either engaged or married already. You can use the knowledge of numerology to make your relationship healthier.

Hence, read through, and I am sure you will learn one or two things that will make your relationship more worthwhile. If you feel your relationship is healthy, it can even be better with this numerology tips. You can never know the full potential of your relationship until you are exposed to some new experiences. I am convinced that your experience in your relationship will even be far better than it was before you read this book.

Single but Searching

If you are single but interested in hooking up with a good partner, your knowledge of numerology can guide your steps. The most important thing is to find someone who is romantically compatible with you. I don't think I need to preach a sermon to you on the importance of compatibility in a relationship. You may claim to be in love with a person initially, but if you are not compatible with the person, the relationship will fizzle out.

So many people who end up breaking up a relationship had felt they were in love at one point but ended up breaking up the relationship. Hence, if you have plans to fall in love and "stay in love," you need to build a relationship on the right foundation. You cannot afford to build your relationship on only physical attraction because it won't stand the test of time. Physical attraction will bring you together initially, but what sustains a relationship is friendship.

Meanwhile, friendship in a relationship is not possible in the absence of compatibility. You and your partner must complement yourselves to avoid having issues that will be classified as "irreconcilable" in the future. I am sure that you don't want to experience the heartache of breaking up with someone you had taught would be your Mr. or Mrs. Right later. Hence, it is always better to start on the right note.

Starting on the right note means that you have to consider the compatibility of you and the person before allowing your emotions to run wide. The best way to do this is to find your **Expression or Psyche number**. Your Psyche Number can be derived from your birth date. It is gotten from the addition of the day, month, and year of your birth. Check chapter five for a better explanation of the importance of your birth date and how to calculate it.

Romantic Compatibility for Searching Singles

Once you know your Psyche Number, you will have a better understanding of your own capabilities and deficiencies. The resultant effect of this knowledge is that you will be able to know people whose Psyche Number is compatible with yours when it comes to a marital relationship. You will have to know the Psyche Number of the person you intend to date also before you can know whether or not the person is compatible with you.

Number 1

If your Psyche Number is 1, you have a kind and disciplined personality. You have an air of authority and can be arrogant. Hence, a person with Psyche Number 2, 3, and 9 are the best for you. A person with Psyche Number 2 is okay with being given instructions. Such people are submissive and will not have serious issues with being bossed around by Number 1s. A person with Psyche Number 3 will be a loyal friend and likes to teach others.

The loyalty and patience of Number 3s make them perfect partners for a Number 1. They will help Number 1 make better decisions in all facets of life. Number 9s are also ideal partners for Number 1s because they offer valuable partnership and friendship. Their positive energy levels will compensate for the tendency of a Number 1 to be rude and abrasive. If you are a Number 1, and you go ahead to date another Number 1, there will be "two captains in a boat." Two number of 1s dating themselves will soon annoy themselves and break up eventually because of their tendency to be bossy.

Number 2

If your Psyche Number is 2, your best chance of building a solid and lasting relationship is with a 1, 3, or another Number 2. A number 1 will support you and be a "pillar" for your soft, tender, and loving nature. A Number will be glad that you don't lord things over him or her and will, in response, offer you maximum support. A Number 3 will reciprocate your friendship, and you will connect on a philosophical level. Another Number 2 will also suit you because your characteristics are alike. Unlike in the case of two Number 1s, two Number 2s are romantically compatible.

Number 3

As a Number 3, you are friendly, spiritual, hard-working, and independent. You are ambitious, just like number 1s, and that is an important connection. You are more practical than Number 1s, and that will make you capable of helping them execute their ideas practically. Your discipline and focus, just like Number 1s, will make you compatible with them. You will also be compatible with a Number 2.

Though they are not as ambitious as 3, their quality support will make them a good business or life partner for you. Your relationship with a Number 9 will also be productive. The organization skills and industry of a Number 9 will attract you, which makes both of you compatible.

Number 4

If you are a Number 4, your rebellious and secretive nature makes you compatible with a number 2 or 8. A number 5 will offer you good friends, but he or she will not be a life partner. Your secrets will be safe with a Number 5, but you can never be sure of what he or she is thinking, and this unpredictability will not be healthy for you. A Number 2 will be a good option for you because of their calm and tender personality.

The calm nature of a Number 2 will be a perfect foil for your turbulent nature. Just like Number 2, Number 8 is also calm and peaceful, and that will make them good partners for Number 4s. 8s can help 4s channel their extreme energies to something positive, thereby making both of them compatible for a marital relationship.

Number 5

As a Number 5, you have an intellectual and entertaining personality. The mental strength of 1s will make them good business partners and friends but not marriage partners. The restlessness of a 5 makes them good friends to 4s, but they will be hindrances to themselves when it comes to a marital relationship. Number 6s are the best life partners for Number 5s. 6s will help 5s get rid of their restlessness because of their loving and caring nature.

Number 6

6s are diplomatic and polite, and you will be forgiven to assume that they will be good partners for 1s. However, that is not the case because their tendency to be slow will not make 1s happy. 4s, 5s, and 8s are ideal life partners for 6s. 4s restlessness will not be an issue for 6s because they will be there to make them calm and channel their energy positively. 4s are similar to 5s in terms of their turbulent nature, and that will make them good options for 6s as well.

8s will make good life partners for 6s because of their calm and spiritual nature. The tendency of 6s to be too social will also be controlled by the calm and intelligent approach of 8s.

Number 7

7s are inventive and intuitive. They are often unrealistic and mystical in their approach to life. The discipline of 1s and the practical approach of 9s to life make 1s and 9s good life partners for 7s. 2s will also be good life partners for 7s, but they will be financial disasters if they partner in business. Both 2s and 7s are not active and disciplined enough to make quality business decisions. The intellectual capability of 7 makes them attractive to and compatible with 8s.

Number 8

If you are a number 8, you should consider dating a 1 or 2. Your hardworking, intellectual, and visionary personality will appeal to a 1. Though both 8s and 1s are egoistic, the positive energy of 8s is a welcome "disinfectant" for the often negative energy of 1s. The supporting cast personality of 2s makes them good life partners for 8s. However, an 8 may feel a 2 is not industrious enough for him or her.

Number 9

Number 9s are realistic, disciplined, and mentally tough. However, they have short tempers and tend to discriminate against people. Their discipline and mental strength will make them good partners for 1s both in business and marital relationships. The realism of 9s also makes them beneficial to number 7s who can be stuck in their own dream world. Both 5s and 9s will generate good positive energy together, which makes them also compatible.

What You Need For A Healthy Relationship

For vain and materialistic people, the answer to a healthy relationship is dating a rich guy or lady. Well, building a healthy relationship goes beyond the financial capabilities of the two parties involved. After reading through the compatibility for singles through numerology, you may feel you are in a relationship. However, you don't have to break your relationship because of the incompatibility of your Psyche Number.

The truth is that you will have issues abound, but no issues are irreconcilable. Never forget that even if you are in a relationship with someone whose Psyche Number is compatible with yours, there will still be issues that both of you will have to learn to solve and grow together. Therefore, being in a relationship with someone whose Psyche Number resonates with yours does not guarantee anything. It only means that you have a higher chance of building a strong and healthy relationship together.

Therefore, people who are in a relationship with someone whose Psyche Number correlates have a lot of work to do to make the relationship work. If they are not careful, they will find out that people who are not compatible based on their natural attributes will have more successful relationships than them. Hence, as much as it is important to be in a relationship with someone who is compatible with you based on your Psyche Number, understanding the person is more important.

If you are with a 1 who has the natural tendency to be dominating and bossy, if you are a 1 or 8, it can be frustrating. However, since you know that is the kind of person you have, you need to focus more on his or her strength. His or her discipline, focus, and determination to achieve his or her dream should catch your attention. If you learn to value your partner's strength and downplay or overlook his or her deficiency, you are set for a long-lasting relationship.

Even if you are a 1 dating a 2, you will like the fact that he or she is tender and supports you but may not be happy with the level of discipline or ambition of the person. Hence, it should matter more to you that you appreciate the part of your partner you like and be willing to help him or her gets rid of the bad attributes. You may want an easy fix, such as suggesting a change of name to your partner to tweak some of his or her attributes. However, you may successfully get rid of a particular attribute you don't like, but be sure that you will see the manifestation of another negative attribute.

Hence, it is always better you know your partner very well and be willing to help him, or her grow. Love the person unconditionally and be ready to forgive any shortcoming. A healthy relationship is built on genuine affection and understanding. Love does not mean that you will ignore the deficiencies; it means that you will be willing to help the person maximize his or her strength and grow out of his or her defects.

The rate of divorce in the modern world is alarming. A major reason for this high rate of divorce is because people are too quick to change relationships. A lot of people have very unrealistic expectations of relationships. No one is perfect. A long-lasting relationship is a deliberate choice to focus on what your partner can do and overlook what he or she cannot do.

Know Your Lucky Date of Marriage

The last part of this chapter is how you can pick a lucky date of marriage. After you have picked a life partner who is compatible with you, you will have to fix a date for your marriage. As a believer in numerology, you should not be frivolous about the date you pick for your marriage. The date you pick will play a role in the fortune of your marriage in the future. Hence, it is always better to be deliberate about your choice.

Your choice of date of marriage should be based on your Lucky Number. Your Lucky Number is your Life Path Number, and it is a derivative of your birth date. Once you find out your Lucky Number, you are good to go. Pick a date that resonates with your Lucky Number to attract a better future for you and your spouse. Your marriage is the beginning of a new life, which promises a lot of possibilities.

Marriage is not a bed of roses, and you have to be mentally ready for it. There will be challenges to navigate and a lot of pleasant moments too. Choosing a wedding date that is in consonance is a good way to start this new life with your partner. You can explain your reason for picking that date to your partner in case of any objection. Dialogue is important in marriage to build a lasting relationship. Hence, if you let your partner be aware of your faith in the power of numbers from the onset, he or she will not term it as unnecessary superstition later on.

However, if you feel your partner is not matured enough or ready for the information, you need not bother him or her for now. You can wait until when you are convinced that he or she can handle the information correctly before explaining how the number influences our experiences as humans on earth. A successful marriage is not impossible or too difficult. The only issue is that many people are not willing to pay the price to get it right.

Chapter 9: Establish Your Business Based On Your Lucky Number

The joy of every businessman or woman is to make a profit. However, making a profit in business is not automatic; you need to be deliberate about it. In other words, you need to take practical steps to ensure that you succeed in business. I don't need to bore you with general principles such as getting your products and services across to the right market or creating a plausible business strategy. You probably know all these before now.

However, if you don't, it is important you understand general foundational business techniques before you invest your money. I know you are eager to know how you can establish your business based on your lucky number. However, I need to be sincere with you here. The knowledge of numerology does not **automatically** mean that you will succeed in any sphere of life, including business. What the knowledge of the power of numbers does for you is to give you an edge in life.

Some believers in numerology are now either pessimists or critics. Why? Their perception of the edge numerology gives people in life was wrong. They expected numerology to take care of the basic aspects of their lives that were meant to be their responsibility. Hence, they felt disappointed and lost hope in the ability of the numbers in their lives to help them live a happy and fulfilled life.

Numerology helps you channel your energy and resources in the right direction. Hence, in this chapter, as I take you through how you can establish your business based on your lucky number, have it in mind that you also need to put in the hard work. This knowledge will make your chances of success higher and not an automatic ticket to becoming successful in your business.

Numerology to the Rescue!

You need to be confident in your chances of becoming a success in your business. Hence, as you start your new business, remove every apprehension or anxiety from your mind, and tell yourself you will succeed. It is okay to be a little bit anxious because you are investing a lot of time, effort, energy, and finance into the business, and you don't want it all to be in vain. However, it is a problem when anxiety begins to impair your performance.

You need not be afraid; numerology has answers to help you become a money magnet. I am sure you are happy to hear that. All that you need to succeed has been deposited in you by the Universe already. Within your core numbers lies the secret of your success. Hence, the knowledge numerology comes in handy to help you marshal your business towards unprecedented success and progress. Financial independence is not elusive for people who are able to walk within the confines of the path the universe has laid down for them.

First things First

The first thing you need to do to establish your business based on your Lucky Number is to find out the number. You don't need a fortune-telling expert to help you with that. If you have been paying attention so far, you should know by now that your Lucky Number is your Life Path Number. Your Life Path number is derived by adding all the values attached to the alphabets in your name together, which will give you a double-digit number. Reduce the double-digit number to a single-digit number by adding the two digits together. There you go!

Now that you know your Lucky Number, you are ready to select the appropriate business name for your new business. In the world of numerology, you cannot afford to take anything for granted. Your business name has to resonate with your lucky number to give you an edge to succeed in your business. In other words, your business name goes a long way in determining whether you will succeed or not. Fortune or stagnation in your business can be altered by simply tweaking the business name to the one that is in alignment with your Lucky Number.

If you already have a business name and have started the business already, it is not too late. If you find out that your business is not yielding as much profit as your hard work deserves, you need to do something fast. I believe what matters to you is the profit and not the name of the business. Hence, if a business name is not helping you realize your potential in business, a little or major tweak to it to maximize profit is a no-brainer. You don't need to convince anyone about the reason for your actions as long as it is the right action.

It is normal that there will be people who will criticize you because they don't understand you, but you need to stand your ground and do what you must do. Hence, when it comes to both minor and major decisions in your life that will turn your life around positively, you need to be more concerned about how the decision affects you. The end justifies the means, after all. Hence, if you are convinced changing your business name will change your fortune in the right direction, why not?

Why does it Matter?

Any right-thinking person must have a reasonable reason for his or her actions. I don't mean that the reason has to be reasonable to others; at least, it has to be reasonable to the person. Hence, it is important that I give you tangible reasons why you need to establish your business based on your Lucky Number. You may think that the reason is obvious because your Lucky Number will help you attract the right people for business, which will, in turn, lead to more profit. However, it goes beyond mere attracting the right people or attracting the right deals.

When you find out your Life Path Number, you will be able to know your strengths and weaknesses. This discovery is particularly important and beneficial if you are yet to start a business. Hence, before you even think about a business name, you would have known the career path that is best for your abilities. In other words, you will know the best business that maximizes your strength and can cope with your deficiencies.

Your life Path Number will also help you determine the kind of people you will have in your business team. You will only recruit people who can be cooperative and supporting such that they will be able to help you achieve your objective. You may not be able to apply this rule to everyone you employ in your company. However, you have to be careful about the people you have in your inner circle. Hence, for such people, you should be concerned about their Life Path Numbers so that you will not have people who will rebel against you or betray you.

Should I be an Entrepreneur or Employee?

Knowing your Life Path number will unveil to you whether you are better off working for others or starting up your own business in the first place. It sounds ridiculous in the modern world today, where almost everyone wants to be a business mogul or tycoon who owns several business chains. It is a good ambition, and anyone who achieves that will be glad. However, it is one thing to dream; it is one thing to have the capacity to achieve the dream.

For example, people who have number 1 as their life path number have leadership qualities such as a strong determination, independence, creativity, and boldness that makes them better entrepreneurs. They can pioneer a business successfully, especially when they are able to reduce the impact of their weaknesses, which include impatience and selfishness. Hence, if your Life Path Number is 1, you are good to go as regards becoming a business owner.

People whose Life Path Number is 2 are cooperative, warm, and diplomatic. They can be entrepreneurs too because of their people skills, but they are better team players. Their attributes are best suited in a business sense when they are part of a company's board. They will always ensure that they don't allow their sentiments get in the way of the objectives of the company. Besides, their tendency to have low self-esteem will be masked when they are not the ones calling the shots. Hence, if your Lucky Number is 2, it will be better if you find someone or people with a vision and mission for a business that resonates with them and helps them succeed. Your invaluable contribution in itself is a success for you.

It is better to be a successful "supporting cast" than become a disaster while playing the leading role. The problem is that most people are not realistic. No one can succeed alone. Every great people in this world, whether in business or another sphere of life were able to succeed because of people who were willing to be at the background of their success. The world is designed in such a way that we cannot all be a protagonist. Some people have to lead while others support them.

Any leader without quality support will crumble. Hence, those in the leading role must be humble enough to acknowledge the effort of those willing to sacrifice for them to succeed. In the same way, those playing the supporting roles must be happy to do it without envying the leader. Why some famous business dynasty crumbled is because they had people who were not happy with their roles who wanted to take the place of the leaders.

True success in life is living a happy and fulfilled life and not necessarily being in the Forbes list. Fame and wealth are good and must be desired. However, the key to living a happy and meaningful life is living life, knowing that you are doing something that offers you the opportunity for maximum expression of your capabilities. If owning a business allows you to maximize your strength and diminish your weaknesses, why not? However, if being part of a successful business team offers you maximum expression, don't be desperate about leading a business team.

I am not in any way discouraging you from achieving your dream of owning business chains (if you have such ambition), I am only more concerned about your happiness because that is what matters the most. Besides, you are still somewhat a business owner if you buy shares from a company because that makes you a stakeholder in the company. Therefore, you have a part to play in the decision making of the company. Hence, your path to fame and wealth is not limited to being a pioneer of a business. You can grow your money via investment in a working business model and still smile at the bank.

Life Path Number 1 Only?

It is important to know that I am not saying that the only people that can succeed as business owners are people whose Life Path Number is 1. I will not be accurate to make such an assertion because it is not true. People with Life Path Number 4 will also make good leaders because of their affinity for orderliness. They are steady, self-disciplined, logical, and orderly. These attributes are essential in leadership. However, they will have to watch out for their tendency to be perfectionists and too demanding.

People with Life Path Number are visionary and resourceful, which are good for leadership, but their tendency to be disorganized, irresponsible, and unstable is not good for business owners. 6, just like 2, is also a better team player rather than a leader. People with this Life Path Number are compassionate and responsible. People with Life Path Number 8 have the best attributes for business. They are ambitious, courageous, and influential. They have all the necessary ingredients to succeed as business owners even above people with Life Path Number 1.

However, they have to be careful to avoid being greedy and materialistic. They have the tendency to sacrifice the happiness of others for their own selfish gain. They also need to be careful about arrogance and the tendency to want to control others. These attributes of Life Path Number 8 inspires a lot of people to change their names or business names such that it will resonate with this number. Such people have to be careful because they cannot accept the positives that come with the Life Path Number 8 and totally reject the negative attributes associated with it.

Best Business Based on Lucky Numbers

Since your Life Path Number reveals your positive and negative attributes, it also helps you know the best business for you. You will struggle if you choose a career path that does not maximize your strength and diminish your defects, you will feel like a fish on dry land; you will be out of sorts. For example, if your Life Path Number is 3, you will thrive more in a business that allows you to be creative and display your magical use of words.

Hence, a career in creative and verbal art will be better for you. Within your core attributes is a good sense of humor. Hence, a career as a public speaker or acting will suit you the most. Your tendency to talk too much will not be obvious in such careers because you are paid to talk after all. Hence, no one will notice your defect, unlike when you find yourself in a career that demands temperance and orderliness.

If your Life Path Number is 4, your affinity for orderliness and discipline will make you thrive in a career like the military. Your resilience and perseverance will come in handy in a career like that, and your inability to fit in perfectly in a social setting will not be obvious. If your life Path Number is 6, a medically-related career will suit you. Your natural ability to care and nurture people will stand out in a career like that. The nature of the work is predictable and can be boring, but it suits you well. It would have been a disadvantage elsewhere, but you will be at home in a career like that.

You will be at home in a career where knowledge, analytical skill, and a studious nature are important if your Life Path Number is 7. Your natural ability to also be inventive will make you thrive in engineering or other careers where technological advancement very vital. Your tendency to be withdrawn and calculative will rather be seen as a strength rather than weaknesses in such careers.

Hence, you need to know your Life Path Number so that you will be able to follow a career path that suits your abilities. Even if you want to change your name to get attributes for a different career, it all begins by knowing your Life Path Number in the first place.

The Best Business Strategy Based on Lucky Numbers

If you are convinced that your path in life is to be a business owner based on your Life Path Number, then it is right for me to help you with picking the best name for your business. If you are into a partnership, you also need to convince your partner to know his or her Life Path Number so that both of you can make the necessary alterations in your names together. It is important both of you make the changes together because your fortune is not enough to determine the fate of a business that is not owned by you alone.

Your business partner does not only contribute his or her money to the business; he or she also contributes to his or her luck. After changing the names as necessary, you are ready for the name of the business. If it is a running business, register the Partnership Deed on your lucky day based on your lucky number. Your brand name should also be changed to reflect your lucky number. Just like I have said earlier, you cannot afford to take anything for granted. Every little detail of your business can affect the success of the business. Hence, pay attention to every detail.

You should also look at your meeting days. As much as it is within your power, ensure you have your business meetings on days that resonate with your lucky number. For your brand color, too, go for colors whose names resonate with your lucky number. It may sound ridiculous, but a detail such as brand color, which you may want to underrate, goes a long way in determining the kind of deals you attract.

Hence, your best business strategy in the numerological sense is to establish your business based on your Lucky Number. This may sound basic, but you must be intelligent with the way you tweak the name of your company or brand name. If your business deals in agricultural products, you cannot tweak the name such that it reflects something related to tech or the medical field. The message you want your products and services to pass across to your clients is what matters first.

You cannot afford to confuse your prospective clients because you want your business name to reflect your Lucky Number. Hence, determine the message first before you determine the best name for your company and products. I have said earlier that you need more than luck to succeed in business. Luck only gives you an edge and not the ultimate thing. Hence, you have to be intelligent with the way you go about tweaking your name, your brand name, or company name.

Such mistakes will make you doubt the effectiveness of numerology when you don't achieve the desired result. Hence, the practice of numerology is not for people who cannot think. You have to be deliberate, strategic, positive, and logical to succeed as a businessman or woman who understands the power of numbers.

Chapter 10: In popular Culture

In this chapter, I will take you through some movies and film shows where numerology featured predominantly. Various topics and themes are used in various popular television and films. Ideas such as serial killers or Zombies are common. However, there are also quite a number of movies, and film shows where numerology was either a central or partial theme. In these movies and film shows, the main idea was to show to the audience how people are using the knowledge of numerology to live a meaningful and fulfilled life.

The influence of the media can be positive or negative. When it comes to numerology, the media has dissuaded many people from taking the power of numbers to offer explanations about important questions of life serious. However, thanks to the media, many people have become more interested in finding out the veracity of the claims of numerology. An example of such a positive influence of the media in fostering the knowledge of numerology is the "Davinci Code." The Davinci code made a lot of people become interested in finding out more about practices that have deeper implications in life.

I must confess that in some movies, numerology was not accurately presented. Hence, you will be making a big mistake if you think you already know what numerology is all about because of what you saw in a movie or TV show. However, the intentions of the writers and directors were right. They were able to display that numerology is not an archaic science that has no practical application in the modern world.

These movies and film shows were able to prove that the lives of people can have deeper meanings through the exploration of the knowledge of the magical power of numbers, thereby starring more people to consider numerology as a science that offers tangible answers to some of life's most important questions. I will bore you or overwhelm you if I pick every movie, novel, and film show where numerology was either a central or partial theme. Hence, I have only selected a few that are some of the best around.

The Davinci Code

The Davinci Code is a movie produced based on a book that was written with the same title by Dan Brown in 2003. This movie was produced in 2006, and it really did a lot of good to the awakening of people to the power of numbers. The core themes of the movie include mysticism, spirituality, religion, and the fight for power. The Fibonacci Sequence is one of the most popular number sequences in the world. In Davinci Code, the Fibonacci Sequence was hidden in an interesting way. The Fibonacci Sequence is a number series such that the value of the next number is equal to the sum of the preceding numbers.

The Fibonacci Sequence is approximately the number of the Golden Spiral. The Golden Spiral is found in the universe and in nature in your ear, snail shells, and in pine cones. In the Davinci Code movie, the Fibonacci Sequence was used in a simple but powerful way to unlock a safe. Amidst the thrill, suspense, and drama of the movie, the power of number unfolds dynamically and a major take away from the movie.

In the movie, a professor of religious symbology, Robert Langdon, is the suspect in the murder of Jacques Sauniere. The police found a cipher on the body and began their investigation to fish out the murderer. The investigations lead them to solicit the help of Sir Leigh Teabing, a notable British Historian. Sir Leigh informs the Police that the real Holy Grail can be found in the painting of Leonardo Davinci, The Last Supper. A secret cabal within the Opus Dei was also searching for the true grail to prevent the destruction of Christianity.

The movie and the book were criticized by the Roman Catholic Church as an attack on Christianity. Nonetheless, both the book and the movie went viral. The movie was the second highest-grossing movie in 2006.

Touch TV series

Touch is an American 2-season series produced in 2012. This TV series starring Kiefer Sutherland was originally aired on Fox and was created by Tim Kring. In this series, Sutherland, who played as Martin Bohm, had an interesting relationship with his son, Jake, who was played by David Mazouz. Martin lost his wife during the September 11 attacks in the World Trade Center and had to raise their 11-year old son, Jake alone. Jake was diagnosed with autism, and Martin had a torrid time raising him. He had to move from one job to the other because of the special needs of taking care of his son.

In the movie, Jake does not speak but has a strong affinity for numbers and patterns relating to numbers. He often spends a lot of his time writing them down on his touch-screen tablet or on a notebook or even popcorn kernels. Jake's fascination with numbers gave him the unusual ability to see the "pain of the universe," according to Professor Teller (Danny Glover). Martin realized that his son had been communicating with his with numbers all these while.

He began to follow the leading of his son through numbers and started achieving more positive results in his daily activities. His devotion to Jake was affecting his social service and scrutiny of his ability to retain the custody of his son. Martin saw the gift of his son as an opportunity to make life more meaningful for others and was using it to help people. However, there were corporations (Aster Corps) who had other plans for the gift of Jake. They killed Professor Teller and were trying to lay hold of Jake by forcing the state to relinquish Martin's custody rights.

Touch was short, but the message is clear: there are awesome possibilities to have a better experience as humans through the power of numbers. It was evident from the movie that the universe is communicating with us through numbers. Those who are able to take advantage of this communication have a higher chance of living a happy and fulfilled life. These communications may be through other people, animals, or a spiritual medium.

VALIS

VALIS is a little old because it was written as far back as 1981. Nonetheless, it is one of the best Novels in terms of investigating the power of numbers. VALIS is a science-fiction novel written by American writer Philip K. Dick. The full meaning of VALIS is a Vast Active Living Intelligence System. VALIS is a Gnostic vision of a single aspect of God, according to Dick. The novel is the first of three series of novels, which was never completed owing to the death of the author. It is an interesting novel in which the writer presents his life as one of the characters of the Novel.

According to Dick, there is a transfer of information from an extraterrestrial species and humans via "pink laser beams." The extraterrestrial species use "disinhibiting stimuli" to communicate to humans via symbols, which activate recollection of intrinsic memory. Dick claimed that he was able to recover his son from the claws of death through his alignment with the message from VALIS. He cited that doctors got the diagnosis of his son wrong, but he insisted they carry out another test in which they diagnose his son of inguinal hernia, which could have killed the child if not quickly operated.

In the story, Horselover Fat was convinced that his visions hold the key to understanding the realities of life on earth. Interestingly, the meaning of "Philip" in Greek is "Fond of horses." Also, the German word for "fat" is "dick." Other researchers who shared similar views with him joined him on his journey to investigate the veracity of these matters. VALIS and the Davinci Code have something in common: the use of the Fibonacci Sequence. The Fibonacci Sequence was used in VALIS as the identification signs of a group of people called the "Friends of God."

Number 23

This movie is a psychological thriller starring Jim Carey, albeit in a non-comedic role. It was written by Fernley Philips and directed by Joel Schumacher. In this movie, he was obsessed with a particular novel he believes was written about him. The book was presented to him as a birthday gift by his wife, Agatha (Virginia Madsen). He noticed that there were a lot of strange similarities between the main character of the Novel, Fingerling, and himself.

Jim Carey's character in the movie, Walter Sparrow, believed that the number 23 is deeply connected to his life and will help him have a deeper understanding of his life. This movie featured a glimpse of the number 23 enigma. The number 23 enigma is the belief that every event has a connection to the number 23 or its derivative via permutation. Walter warned his wife about this number, but he didn't make any sense to her, and she told him he was crazy.

He read in the book that Fingerlings murdered his girlfriend, and he started having dreams related to him killing his wife. Walter was referred to Isaac French (Danny Huston), Agatha's friend, who suggested that he should find the author of the book to find the answers he craves. In the movie, the number kept popping up everywhere, both directly and indirectly. It can appear in the form of seeing a staircase with 23 steps or searching for something in room 23 of a hotel.

Sometimes, the number is derived through the use of a simple code by the character in which every letter of the alphabet is numbered from 1 to 26. In that order, a name like "Ned" will equal 23 (14 + 5 + 4). Another important point in the movie was when the main character read every 23rd word in the novel, which helped him locate an address that helps him put the pieces of his lost memory together.

Pi (II)

This movie is the story of a number theorist. The obsession of Max, the protagonist in the movie, to unlock the secret of nature makes him engage in extreme self-destructive behaviors. Max is an unreliable narrator as he suffers from hallucinations and paranoia. He is convinced that numbers explain everything and finds it difficult to make any sense of the patterns in the systems around you.

In the movie, he came across a number, a 216 sequence that seems to make a bold financial prediction. It was initially rejected bur came true. Various lead to the work of Max gaining the attention of a Hassidic group and a Wall Street firm. The Wall Street firm was interested in the financial implication of the number while the Hassidic group believes the number will usher in the messianic age for them. What followed was a paranoid and tense chase causing Max hallucinations and terrible visions that ultimately lead to the loss of all the knowledge of everything Max was trying to find out initially.

There are three main themes in the movie: Kabbalah, the game of go, and mathematics. The Kabbalic theme is seen in how that Pi unveiled the concept of the "Explicit Name." The manipulation of the number 216 letter word will generate 72 columns of the three-letter names of the Hebrew God. The mathematical theme is seen in how Max was able to find a golden spiral showing up wherever he looks. Max believed that any phenomenon could be explained by understanding the mathematics that embodies the golden spiral. The golden spiral is a shape that has been of interest to great scientists, including Pythagoras and Roger Penrose. The growth of the shape is based on the golden ratio.

The game of Go is an ancient game dated as far back as over 2,500 years ago. The complexity that arises from the simple set of rules of the game has always inspired the study of mathematics. In the movie, the characters used the game as a model for their perspective of the universe. They believe that the game is more of a microcosm of the chaotic nature of the world around them.

Numb3rs

Numb3rs TV show reflects the positive role of numerology in the lives of people. This crime drama had six seasons that have the mathematical genius of an FBI agent's brother in focus. The FBI agent's brother uses his mathematical ability to help his brother solve crimes. Every episode of Numb3rs ends in such a way that the FBI agent will end up solving a crime with the aid of the mathematical ingenuity of his brother.

Numb3rs is not without its flaws. For example, it often features unrealistic and questionable mathematical concepts primarily because of the way the script of the drama was written. It is almost as though the plots have been written completely beforehand in such a way that spaces were left for the insertion of mathematical terms that will appeal to the audience before filming, just like the scripts of Star Trek.

Hence, sometimes, there is no link between the mathematical term and the events. However, despite this shortcoming, the characters were able to successfully display how a person can go about the pursuit of the knowledge of numerology personally. Numerology was often portrayed in the film show as a knowledge that can help people have foresight about future events that will unravel in the future. The Gemetria, which is an alphanumeric code of giving words or phrases numerical value based on its letters, was also in extensive use in Numb3rs.

Numerology and Gemetria were used as viable tools for understanding the world around us in the film show. In Numb3rs, the characters were able to pay attention to the patterns in the numerical relationships around them. This awareness of numerical patterns, which helps us to unlock knowledge that was previously hidden, is a major part of numerology. Without any form of mysticism, those who are skillful in numerology will be able to identify these numerical links.

Bee Season

This movie was adapted from a book whose title is also called "Bee Season." It is an American drama in which the daughter of a perpetually dysfunctional family displayed an unexpected knack for winning spelling bees. This newfound success disrupted the dynamic of this family as members of the family begin to discover themselves and have a spiritual awakening as the girl inch closer to winning the national competition.

Numerology is not the major theme in this movie but a part of the lives of the characters who were husband and wife. The husband, played by Richard Gere, is a professor of religious studies who wrote a graduate thesis on the Kaballah. Meanwhile, the wife, played by Juliette Binoche, converted to Judaism after their marriage. She was living a secret life based on her belief in the "tikkun Olam," which is a Kabbalistic belief that humans have a shared responsibility in transforming and repairing the world. "Tikkun Olam" is a Jewish word that means "repairing the world."

Her husband took a special interest in her after realizing that she had inspired her with his own spiritual beliefs. Hence, he began to coach her by employing his Kabbalah techniques. This new interest leads him to pay a lot of attention to his wife at the expense of the children. The key lesson from this movie is how a person can utilize the Kabbalah in everyday living. Though numerology did not play the major part in the plot of the movie, it was a deliberate insight into how a lot of people are using the knowledge of numerology to have a better experience in their lives.

11-11-11

11-11-11 is a horror film written and directed by Darren Lynn Bousman in 2011. It has the number 11 written all over it from the storyline to the release date. It was set at 11:11 on the 11th day in the 11th month and released on November 11, 2011. In the movie, Joseph Crone, a writer, played by Timothy Gibbs dreamt that his wife and son were trapped in their burning home and eventually died. He woke up by 11:11 in his hotel room on November 7, 2011.

Joseph was involved in a car accident on November 8, 2011, that got him hospitalized. His MRI scan showed that he was not hurt, but the driver had died. When he checked his wristwatch, it was 11:11. His brother, Samuel (Michael Landes), called him that night to inform him that their father (Denis Rafter) was dying. Joseph went to see his father the next day in Barcelona, where his brother showed him a security video called "de los demonios." The video showed a faint outline of a demon at 11:11 pm.

Joseph informed Samuel about how he had seen 11-11 frequently recently. Ana, the local housekeeper, informs Joseph based on a diary titled El Libro de Ana, which is the gospel according to her that the number sequence shows that Joseph has been "Activated." Joseph rescued Samuel that night from creatures looking like demons who were trying to strangle Samuel. Joseph later finds a photo in the custody of Javier who had tried to kill Samuel with the words "SACRIFICIO" scribbled on it.

Joseph was convinced that Samuel is a prophet that the demons were trying to kill so that the "Serpent" will rise and birth a new religion after the destruction of the church. However, he was wrong as he found out too late that Samuel was actually the devil that he should have stopped. The movie ends with time in the future when a large congregation was reading a book titled "The Book of Joseph."

Other Worthwhile Mentions

Other works on numerology worth mentioning include XKCD and Harry Potter. XKCD is a famous internet comic serious written by Randall Monroe. Randall Monroe is a former NASA roboticist. This internet sensation that touched on math, science, love, and philosophy made the best use of the Fibonacci Sequence. In Harry Potter, Numerology was practiced in the name of **Arithmancy,** which was an elective course in "Harry Potter and the Prisoner of Azkaban."

FAQ

There are many questions people ask about numerology out of curiosity or pessimism. It is quite difficult for some people to believe that understanding the properties of numbers in their lives can be enough to answer questions about life. Below are frequently asked questions about numerology and the answers:

Is numerology all about mathematics?

For those who do not like mathematics, you don't need to be afraid because numerology is not all about mathematics. Numerology is the science of numbers, and there are aspects where you have to do a mathematical operation like a simple addition when finding your core numbers. Numerology is all about understanding the attributes of numbers and how they affect your life. You don't need to obtain a degree in mathematics before you can successfully understand and practice numerology. Numerology is a deliberate exploration and answer to difficult life questions like your purpose and greatest drive.

Can numerology predict my future?

The answer to this question is "No" because it is not God. However, numerology can help you understand the reasons for the events unraveling themselves in your life. Therefore, numerology can help you know the kind of events that are likely to take place in your life in the future. However, your understanding of the numbers in your life does not automatically mean you will achieve success or fail in the future. The course of your life is determined by the actions you take or did not take.

Are there good and evil numbers?

People who do not understand the properties of numbers in numerology often assume that there are numbers that are inherently positive or negative. However, it is not true that there are numbers that have only positive or negative attributes. In numerology, every number has both positive and negative properties. Hence, before you are hell-bent on changing your name to alter some characteristics or events in your life, you need to think twice. You will have to accept the positive attributes of your core numbers and do your best to limit the negative attributes so that you can have balance in your life.

Is there is a connection between numerology and religion?

No. Numerology is not a religion but a universal science. Numerology is not only about human beings but can even be applicable in the case of animals. Both humans and animals have the date they were born. Hence, numerology helps us understand the positive and negative attributes of both people and animals. In other words, your name or the name you call your pet has both positive and negative attributes in numerology. Numerology is the knowledge of the energy of the vibration energies of numbers and not a religion.

What kind of answers does numerology answer?

Numerology helps you to understand who you are, your path in life, your motivation, and your direction. Questions about your personality, strengths, and weaknesses are all answered through the knowledge of numerology. Numerology can help you know your natural talents and the best career path that suits your characteristics. You can also know the right person to marry, the kind of business you can invest, and the kind of location that is best for you. You can know when you need to be patient and when you need to make changes in your life through the knowledge of numerology.

Can I know my soul mate through the knowledge of numerology?

Yes! You can know whether your current relationship is the right one through the knowledge of numerology. Your Life Path Number reveals your purpose, strength, and weakness. Hence, you can determine whether you are romantically compatible with a person or not when you know the Life Path Number of the person. You can know whether the person's strength complements your weaknesses and vice versa. Hence, numerology can help you know who to avoid and who you should give a chance to win your heart and stay in your life.

What is the difference between numerology and astrology?

Astrology deals with the movement of planetary bodies and their effects on our lives. Astrology is quite rigid and unchangeable because you cannot alter the movement of planetary bodies. However, in numerology, you can alter the events in your life by altering your name. At its peak, astrology is like a mirror. You can see yourself and your features, but you can do nothing but to accept the image presented to you by the mirror. However, numerology is like plastic surgery. If there are aspects of your life you are not comfortable with, you can make alterations in numerology to have new experiences.

Is numerology all about my date of birth?

Numerology is not concerned about your date of birth alone. It is easy to think numerology will only utilize your date of birth because it contains numbers. However, your birth name and the name people call you are also of importance in numerology. Your full name can be converted to digits through the addition of values that are assigned to the letters that make up your name.

Is Nameology the same as Numerology?

"Nameology" is a part of a whole while numerology is the whole. Nameology is the analysis of name vibrations based on values in numerology. Numerology helps you to understand how the numbers in your name affect your life both positively and negatively.

What is the importance of my name in numerology?

Your name determines the positive and negative experiences you will have in life. Therefore, your name plays a very important role in numerology. When people change their names because of unfortunate reasons such as a divorce, it is a big deal in numerology. When the name is converted to a digit in numerology, the attributes of the old and new name is not likely to be the same. Hence, your name says a lot about you in a numerological context. Hence, you have to be careful before you change your name because it may change your fortune.

Conclusion

What a journey! I am convinced that every doubt and question you have about numerology should have been resolved by now. It is okay to have your doubts about numerology because you are an intelligent person. Intelligent people don't just accept whatever they are told until they have verified it for themselves. There is lots of propaganda and false things appearing or claiming to be true out there. Hence, it is normal for you to want to be double sure before you believe in the veracity of numerology. Your desire to find out things for yourself must have convinced you to purchase this book in the first place.

Unfortunately, some people dismiss numerology without verifying their claims. Such people will never know what they are missing until they somehow change their minds and check out the authenticity of the claims of numerology. I am glad that you made the decision to take a leap of faith to find out if numbers indeed have the answer to important questions of life. I am sure by now that you are happy to have committed your energy and time to read through this book.

Do more than Reading!

It is good that you have read the book, but you should do more than that. You have to practice what you have read. Unfortunately, so many people read books for the sake of amassing more knowledge. Some read wide so that whenever there is an argument, they will be able to contribute without feeling like a fish out of water. However, if you read a book like this and you didn't take it to the next level to practice, it is all futile. You are not better than people who don't believe that numerology is real if you have the knowledge, but don't put it to use.

In fact, pessimists and critics of numerology are better than you if you are not taking advantage of the knowledge of numerology to improve your life. At least, such people will not waste their time and effort on reading something like this. In the long run, you will have the same kind of experiences and uncertainty they have in life in spite of your knowledge. The fact that you are working in a soap industry does not automatically mean you will be clean. You have to take the soap and take your bath with it before you can be clean.

In the same way, reading a book on numerology does not automatically mean you will enjoy the benefits of understanding the magical power of numbers. You have to apply your knowledge to every area of your life before you can enjoy the benefits of having the knowledge of numerology. Nothings come your way on a platter of gold in life; you have to show that you are ready to do what is necessary to make things work before you can succeed in life. You have to be deliberate about changing your life if you truly want to have new positive experiences.

For example, I don't expect that you won't know your core numbers by now! You should have calculated and known your Life Path number, Expression Number, and Soul Urge number by now. The best time you should practice whatever you are learning in life is immediate. When you procrastinate, you will start losing the enthusiasm you had initially when you first received the knowledge. Over time, the knowledge will become stale, and you may even start doubting the veracity and relevance of the knowledge.

If the reason you are yet to practice what you have been learning in this book is that you wanted to wait until you are done, it is okay. It is not too late to make amends. The first thing you need to do is to calculate your core numbers. Once you know your core numbers, find out the meaning of those numbers and how they reveal your identity. Discover your personality and your capabilities. Identify your weaknesses and start working on how you can curb them to live a happy and fulfilled life.

Live a Happy and Fulfilled Life!

The ultimate reason this book was written is to improve your experience in life. In other words, this book was written to help you live a happy and fulfilled life. Therefore, if you know your Life Path Number, Expression Number, Lucky Number, Soul Urge Number, and Destiny number but fail to live a happy and fulfilled life, the objective of this book is not fulfilled. Every chapter of the book was deliberately filled with information that will improve your life.

I have done my best to provide you with accurate information that will make you make the best decisions through your knowledge of numerology. Hence, the ball is in your court. No one else apart from you can decide whether you will live a happy life or not apart from you. Every area of your life can experience a tremendous turnaround if only you want it to be so. You can make the right choice about your career path because you understand your natural talents. You know you're your strengths and weaknesses and the best career that suits your capabilities.

You can make the right choice martially because you now know people who will not be suited for you. Hence, you will not only consider how beautiful or cute a person is; you will look at the person's compatibility with you. You will be able to make the right choices about where you live because you know that your address affects the positive and negative experiences you have.

Hence, it will be a major disaster if you end up not living a happy and fulfilled life in spite of all these "weapons" you have.

It will mean that you have chosen not to "fight" when you have all you need to win. I believe you will not let me down; you will make use of the invaluable information you have received. Not doing so is ultimately letting you down.

References

Bullinger E. W. (1921). Number in Scripture. Eyre & Spottiswoode (Bible Warehouse) Ltd.

Campbell F. (1931). Your Days Are Numbered: A Manual of Numerology for Everybody. DeVorss & Company. ISBN 0-87-516422-6.

Drayer R.A. (2002). Numerology, The Power in Numbers, A Right & Left Brain Approach. ISBN 0-9640321-3-9.

Five types of numerology - Patristic Center. (n.d.). Retrieved October 20, 2019, from http://www.patristiccenter.org/five-types-of-numerology/

Hans, D. (2017). Single-Digit Numbers. Retrieved October 22, 2019, from

https://www.worldnumerology.com/numerology-single-digit-numbers.htm

Hans, D. (2017). Master Numbers. Retrieved October 19, 2019, from

https://www.worldnumerology.com/numerology-master-numbers.htm

Hans, D. (2017). Karmic Debt Number in Numerology. Retrieved October 24, 2019, from https://www.worldnumerology.com/numerology-karmic-debt.html

Hans, D. (n.d.-c). Numerology Compatibility | Numerology.com. Retrieved October 24, 2019, from https://www.numerology.com/numerology-news/numerology-compatibility-life-path-number

Hans, D. (n.d.-a). Expression Numbers | Numerology.com. Retrieved October 23, 2019, from https://www.numerology.com/numerology-news/expression-number-numerology

Kari, S. (n.d.). Numerology for Your Address – Is Your Home Happy for You? Retrieved October 19, 2019, from https://karisamuels.com/home-numerology/

Milton, B. (2013, March 11). Numerology in popular culture. Retrieved October 23, 2019, from

https://sapientparadox.wordpress.com/2013/03/12/numerology-in-

popular-culture/

Nagy A. M. (2016). Numerology Workbook: using Chaldean Mysticism

(Paperback).

Pochat W. & Pirmaïer M. (2011). The Unveiled Numerology – vol. 1 – You do not

necessarily carry the name you think.

Sara, C. (2018, October 26). Meaning of Life Path Number. Retrieved October 22,

2019, from https://www.refinery29.com/en-us/life-path-number-

numerology-meaning

Schimmel A. (1993). The Mystery of Numbers (a scholarly compendium of the

connotations and associations of numbers in historical cultures). New

York, USA: Oxford University Press. ISBN 0-87-516422-6.

Terry, F. (2016, October 31). "Extremely lucky" phone numbers could fetch B100

million. Retrieved October 21, 2019, from

https://www.bangkokpost.com/learning/advanced/1123520/-extremely-lucky-phone-numbers-could-fetch-b100-million

The Types of Numerology. (n.d.). Retrieved October 16, 2019, from

http://www.spiritlink.com/kinds.html

The Connection Between Numerology And Astrology. (n.d.). Retrieved October 17, 2019, from https://www.astroyogi.com/articles/the-connection-between-numerology-and-astrology.aspx

A SPIRITUAL START!

Start your week with gratitude, joy, inspiration, and love. Healing, motivation, inspiration, challenge and guidance straight to your inbox every week!

FIND OUT MORE

www.ingramcontent.com/pod-product-compliance
Lightning Source LLC
Chambersburg PA
CBHW021818060426
42554CB00046B/836